The TIME of YOUR LIFE

In Light of Eternity

STEVE GALLAGHER

The TIME *of* YOUR LIFE

In Light of Eternity

STEVE GALLAGHER

ALSO AVAILABLE BY STEVE GALLAGHER:

At the Altar of Sexual Idolatry
The Walk of Repentance
Living in Victory
Irresistible to God
Out of the Depths of Sexual Sin
A Biblical Guide to Counseling the Sexual Addict
How America Lost Her Innocence
Intoxicated with Babylon
A Lamp Unto My Feet
Pressing On Toward the Heavenly Calling
Create in Me a Pure Heart
Standing Firm through the Great Apostasy
He Leads Me Beside Still Waters

For these books and other resources please contact:
PURE LIFE MINISTRIES
14 School Street
Dry Ridge, KY 41035
(888) PURELIFE - to order
(859) 813-0005 FAX
www.purelifeministries.org

THE TIME OF YOUR LIFE:
In Light of Eternity

ISBN 0-9800286-5-5
EAN 978-0-9800286-5-2

BIBLE TRANSLATIONS *(in order of usage)*

1. **NASB** – NEW AMERICAN STANDARD BIBLE®, Copyright © 1960, 1962, 1963, 1971, 1972, 1973, 1975, 1977, 1995 by The Lockman Foundation. Used by permission (www.Lockman.org).
2. **LB** – *The Living Bible*, Copyright © 1971 by Tyndale House Publishers, Wheaton, IL.
3. **PHP** – J.B. Phillips, *The New Testament in Modern English* (Revised Edition), Copyright © 1996 by Touchstone Publishing, Austin, TX.
4. **MSG** – *The Message*, Copyright © 1993, 1994, 1995, 1996, 2000, 2001, 2002 by Eugene H. Peterson. Used by permission of NavPress Publishing Group.
5. **Amp** – *Amplified® Bible*, Copyright © 1954, 1958, 1962, 1964, 1965, 1987 by The Lockman Foundation. Used by permission (www.Lockman.org).
6. **Dar** – *The Holy Scriptures: A New Translation from the Original Languages*, Copyright © 1996 by Logos Research Systems, Inc., Oak Harbor, WA.
7. **KJV** – *The King James Version, (The Authorized Version)*, Public Domain.
8. **NLT** – *Holy Bible, New Living Translation*, Copyright © 1996, 2004. Used by permission of Tyndale House Publishers, Inc., Wheaton, IL 60189. All rights reserved.
9. **NEB** – *The New English Bible*, Copyright © 1961, 1970 by The Oxford University Press and the Syndics of the Cambridge University Press.
10. **Mof** – *The Moffatt Translation of the Bible*, Copyright © 1972 by Hodder & Stoughton Ltd., St. Paul's House, London, England.
11. **WNT** – *Weymouth's New Testament in Modern Speech*, Copyright © 1987 by Lutterworth Press Cambridge, UK.
12. **GNB** – *Good News Bible*, Copyright © 1966, 1971, 1976, 1992 by American Bible Society. Used by Permission.
13. **NET** – *The NET Bible®*, Copyright © 2005 by Biblical Studies Press, L.L.C. accessed at www.netbible.com. All rights reserved.
14. **NIV** – *The Holy Bible: New International Version* (electronic edition), Copyright © 1996, 1984 by Zondervan Grand Rapids, MI.
15. **BBE** – *Bible in Basic English*, Public Domain.
16. **Knox** – *The Holy Bible: A Translation from the Latin Vulgate of the Hebrew and Greek Originals* by Monsignor Ronald Knox, Copyright © 1954. Special thanks to www.cormacburke.or.ke for providing the text online.
17. **Hol** – *The Holy Bible: Holman Christian Standard Version*, Copyright © 2003 by Holman Bible Publishers, Nashville, TN.
18. **NKJV** – *New King James Version*, Copyright © 1979, 1980, 1982 by Thomas Nelson, Inc. Used by permission. All rights reserved.
19. **Wuest** – *The New Testament: An Expanded Translation*, Copyright © 1994 by Wm. B. Eerdmans Publishing Company, Grand Rapids, MI.
20. **GDBY** – William Baxter Godbey, New Testament, 1902, Public Domain, accessed at http://www.e-swordfiles.com.
21. **Har** – *The Psalms for Today: A New Translation from the Hebrew into Current English*, by R.K. Harrison as quoted in *Norlie's Simplified New Testament*, Copyright © 1961 by Zondervan Publishing House.
22. **GSPD** – *The New Testament: An American Translation*, Copyright © 1923, 1948 by The University of Chicago Press, Chicago, IL.

DEDICATION

I dedicate this book to Adam, Dave, Greg, Jeff, Jim and Tom who were there for me in my time of need. May God richly bless each of you for what you mean to Kathy and me.

THE TIME OF YOUR LIFE
In Light of Eternity

PROLOGUE

I t was January 21, 2011 and Juanita Rex was about to enter the most anguish-filled and glorious three days of her life. It was painful, because she was watching Eunice, her 81-year-old mother, in the throes of death. The woman who had loved her unconditionally and taught her how to live the unselfishness of the Christian life was now in the final moments of life. What was particularly difficult was watching the convulsions that would wrack her feeble frame. "Oh God, please make it stop!" Juanita would cry out inside. "Please take her home!"

These intermittent seizures would have been too much for Juanita to bear were it not for what transpired between them. For what she witnessed as her mother lingered here in her earthly body was the most astonishing sense of the eternal realm she had ever experienced. It was very obvious that, in some inexplicable way, her mother was living in both worlds at the same time; or perhaps her soul kept drawing near to heaven while her body continued to cling to earth life. All Juanita knew was that the atmosphere of ineffable peace that filled that hospital room could only have come from another realm.

"The trees are so beautiful," Eunice said, waking up from

a time of quiet slumber. "I can hear the birds!"

After one particularly violent episode of muscle spasms, Juanita thought to encourage her mother. "Mother, you're going to have a mansion in heaven!"

"I saw it!" Eunice exclaimed. "I saw my mother and father, too. Oh, Juanita, it's so wonderful!"

On another occasion, Juanita could sense that her mother had something very urgent to say. Struggling between spasms, she said, "Praise God for the victory. I have eternal life." After quoting John 3:16, *For God so loved the world, that He gave His only begotten Son, that whoever believes in Him shall not perish, but have eternal life,* with a quiet but mighty unction she said, "This means *everyone* who believes. And whoever doesn't, God will condemn."

Juanita was astounded by this final statement because it was so out of character for her. Eunice was a quiet woman who simply accepted people as they were and didn't think in those terms. And yet, there was no mistaking the implication of her words and the authority with which they were spoken.

In one of their final moments together, Eunice looked at her daughter earnestly, and, gripping her hand tightly, said, "Juanita, preach the Gospel. Tell the world that Jesus saves. Tell it to the generations to come. Trust in God, stay faithful to the end. It's worth it all. I am going to heaven. Tell all of our loved ones that I want to see them there."

A few hours later her soul emerged from the tunnel of Time and entered another world—a glorious world—that would be hers to enjoy forevermore.*

Perhaps the words of that old hymn would best describe what Eunice saw laying just over the hilltop for herself:

> *Shall we gather at the river,*
> *Where bright angel feet have trod,*

---

* This story was related to me by Karla Buch, Juanita's sister and a close personal friend of mine.

With its crystal tide forever
Flowing by the throne of God.
Yes, we will gather at the river,
The beautiful, the beautiful river;
Gather with the saints at the river
That flows by the throne of God.

Soon we'll reach the shining river,
Soon our pilgrimage will cease;
Soon our happy hearts will quiver,
With the melody of peace.[1]

INTRODUCTION

There is one commodity that every living being has been granted: Time. Although the amount may vary, we have all been given enough time on earth for our hearts to be tested, our lives to be judged and our eternities to be determined. This entire probationary process occurs within the great realm of Time.

Time is both objective and subjective. On one hand, it operates as an unseen measuring tool as God unfolds His grand, all-encompassing purposes for earthbound mankind.

And yet on the other hand it is something that is very personal to you and me. Our past existence and future hopes are distinctive to ourselves. The Lord has granted each of us a specific period to live out the life He has given to us. How will we use this valuable resource? What kind of fruit will it bear in our lifetimes? What lies ahead for us after we transition from "this present age" into "the age to come?"

Man is immortal and therefore the subject of Time is of enormous importance. It affects every aspect of our lives. It is vital that we understand its value, utilize it wisely and prepare for its long-term existence. In one of His parables, Jesus used the monetary term "talent" to illustrate the spiritual resources available to the believer which he is expected to employ on behalf of his Master's interests on earth. Certainly time must be one of those resources.

I believe that a study on such a subject as time must be done wholly from a spiritual standpoint; after all, when it's all said and done, nothing else will matter. I know of one Christian philosopher who wrote a book on the subject; but it seems to me to be an awkward attempt at aligning biblical concepts he has embraced with the godless logic of the scientific community. He even suggested that anyone wishing to learn about the subject of eternity would be better off studying the writings of a Christian philosopher (such as himself) than those of theologians. Personally, I would rather hear from a man who has been touched by the Eternal than one who approaches spiritual concepts merely through his mental acumen—whether his study is built upon a philosophical or theological foundation. Joseph Parker said it this way:

> He who does not know God has no key with which to open anything; he is in the midst of ten thousand cabinets each of which contains gold and rubies and all manner of gems, but he has no key. To understand God through love is to understand everything else; then like God we take up the hills as a very little thing and handle constellations as if they were mere toys.[1]

Be that as it may, I have done my best to tackle the subject and to present my findings in (hopefully) a concise and readable form. My hope in this book is to offer the reader a fresh peek into the unseen realm to discern God's mysterious ways at work in our lives; to diminish the value we place on the temporal and enhance the importance of the eternal; to alleviate the fear of death and to instill hope and even excitement about the hereafter.

This book addresses the twin subjects of Time and Eternity along the lines of a typical, Christian life. The first section describes the temporal realm in which sinful mankind lives and out of which the believer is saved. The second describes the Christian's challenge of maintaining an eternal perspective while living in a temporally-minded culture. The third part of the book addresses the spiritual laws that determine a believer's rewards—and even quality of life—in heaven. The last section contemplates what that life in heaven must be like for all who are allowed to live there.

As part of this project, I felt it necessary to provide the reader some additional study material in the form of two appendices.

The first appendix is an attempt to help substantiate certain books written by people who have had visions of or out-of-body experiences in heaven—a subject not addressed until the final section. I definitely encourage you to read it before proceeding into Part Four.

I have also provided a list of quotes and Scriptures that relate to the subjects of Time and Eternity that one can study and meditate upon.

This book is meant to be an enjoyable examination of a subject that deeply affects us all. I trust that you will be provoked in your thinking, challenged in your lifestyle and encouraged about your future as you consider *The Time of Your Life in Light of Eternity.*

TIME

Time's a hand's breadth; 'tis a tale;
'Tis a vessel under sail;

'Tis an eagle in its way,
Darting down upon its prey;

'Tis an arrow in its flight,
Mocking the pursuing sight;

'Tis a short-lived fading flower;
'Tis a rainbow on a shower;

'Tis a momentary ray
Smiling in a winter's day;

'Tis a torrent's rapid stream;
'Tis a shadow; 'tis a dream;

'Tis the closing watch of night,
Dying at the rising light;

'Tis a bubble; 'tis a sigh;
Be prepared, O man, to die.

—Fancis Quarles (c. 1600)

Part One:

TEMPORAL LIFE

*"Time is a continual over-dropping of moments,
which fall down one upon the other, and evaporate."*
—Anonymous[1]

"He has planted eternity in the human heart."
—Solomon[2]

ETERNITY IN THE HEART

Mankind lives in the realm of Time.
Time is a major component of the great cosmos in
which everything we know exists. It is a path upon
which we are ever walking. We measure it, keep it, observe it
and submit to it. Time affects every part of our lives.

Our vocabulary continually reflects its importance in our
daily lives. We talk about good times and hard times; prehistoric
times and modern times. We speak of crunch time, bedtime,
small time and the big time. We say we are biding time, pressed
for time, buying time, killing time and taking our time. We
won't give one person the time of day, but we'll give another
the time of their life.

Then there are all those little sayings alluding to time that
don't even mention the actual word: at the drop of a hat, down
to the wire, haste makes waste, in the heat of the moment, a
month of Sundays, around the clock, better late than never,
to the bitter end, in the blink of an eye, in a coon's age, in the
short run, light years ahead, like clockwork and twenty-four-
seven. The truth is we use these idioms and phrases all the
time!

WHAT PRECISELY IS TIME?

One dictionary defines time as: "A nonspatial continuum in which events occur in apparently irreversible succession from the past through the present to the future."[3]

Another says, "That part of existence which is measured in seconds, minutes, hours, days, weeks, months, years, etc., or this process considered as a whole."[4]

Wikipedia promotes a more scientific line of thought: "Time is part of the measuring system used to sequence events, to compare the durations of events and the intervals between them, and to quantify the motions of objects."[5]

Whatever else may be said about it, it is clear that Time is sequential, meaning that actions and events succeed one another. That means that if we trace Time all the way back to the beginning—as described in Genesis One—every action has occurred consecutively since then. Time is one giant line (or continuum) that contains past, present and future.

On the first day of Creation, the timeline of mankind seemed to stretch endlessly into the future. By the time Christ returns, all Earth's history will have "come and gone." Between these two points, lies everything man has ever done: the significant and petty, the noble and despicable, the dull and exciting.

Human beings live in the present—the Now. At this moment you and I are experiencing life (although, obviously, the writing of this book has occurred at least months prior to your reading it). Those experiences—no matter how mundane or how exciting—slip into our past, moment by moment. Each moment is encountered, experienced and discarded. No sooner has one moment passed than another is there to take its place. This transaction occurs some 86,000 times a day!* An unceasing flow of future moments are constantly streaming toward us.

---

* The number of seconds in 24 hours.

Everything we have done in life trails behind us as some kind of intangible tail. Thoughts we have pondered, words we have spoken and actions we have taken all combine to construct our own personal timelines. When Christians share their testimonies or famous ministers write their autobiographies, they are communicating the events and experiences that have made up their timelines up to that point.

One of the common fallacies is that Time flows from the past, through the present and on into the future. That notion is prevalent because that is the direction of human history: it began in the ancient past, continues through today and will culminate in the future.

But Time actually flows in the opposite direction. We are continually facing the future and moving into it—much like navigating a boat upriver. Time does not originate in the past; it awaits us in the future.

As one writer observed, "Tomorrow becomes today. Today becomes yesterday. The future becomes the present. The present becomes the past. The future is the source, it is the reservoir of time which will some day be present, and then past. The present is the narrow strait, it is the living instant, it is the flashing reality, through which the vast oncoming future flows into the endless receding past."[6]

To illustrate this great truth, consider Billy, a young man looking forward to adulthood. He turns twenty-one on January 20th of the coming year. During the month of December, he excitedly anticipates his big day as arriving "next month," then it will be "next week," then it will be "tomorrow." Finally the momentous day arrives. His family and friends throw a birthday party for him. After all of the festivities are over, Billy falls asleep and wakes up a few hours later to a new day. A week later his big day is well behind him and he has moved on with life. A year later, he can hardly recall the events of that day: they are but a vague memory. He moved toward his 21st birthday, experienced it and then left it in his past.

This sense of Time residing in the future and moving toward the past can be seen in prophecy. For instance, the Lord told Habakkuk: "For the vision is yet for the appointed time; it hastens toward the goal and it will not fail. Though it tarries, wait for it; for it will certainly come, it will not delay." (Habakkuk 2:3)

THE CONCEPT OF TIME IN SCRIPTURE

If time plays such an important part of life, then it should be no surprise that we find it mentioned over and over in Scripture. The truth is that the Bible itself is a timeline of man's existence upon earth and on into the hereafter.[†] In fact, for the most part it is laid out chronologically, so that a person can open the Bible on any given page and find himself examining a specific period of world history.

The book of Genesis covers the longest period of time. Chapter Five alone covers some 1,500 years. By the time of the Exodus, nearly 3,000 years have come and gone. The historical books (Joshua through Esther), the poetical books (Job through Song of Solomon) and the prophetical books (Isaiah through Malachi) communicate the story of the Jewish people through the conquering of Canaan (c.1200 B.C.), the monarchy period (c.1000-586 B.C.), the exile to Babylon and the return to the land (c. 586-538 B.C.). The entire New Testament period occurs within the First Century A.D.

However, it should also be noted that many books point backward to periods of ancient history or forward to the Last Days and on into eternity. For instance, Luke 3 covers the genealogy of Jesus Christ back to Adam, while Luke 21 discusses earth life during the end times. Revelation 12 touches on the great insurrection in heaven (which apparently occurred before Creation), while Revelation 21-22 describes the eternal habitation of the elect.

---

† Scripture is mostly silent about history between the Second and Twentieth Centuries.

In addition to its focus on history, the Bible simply employs a lot of Time terminology. Consider how often the following words are used in Scripture: time (722), age (83), year (748), month (237), day (2,042), hour (85), eternal (80), everlasting (1,063), forever (318), now (2,165) then (3,632), when (2,632), while (456), before (1,434) and after (816). These terms alone (not taking into account the many other words that directly or indirectly relate to time) amount to 53% of the number of verses in the Bible (31,000).

The primary Greek terms translated as "time" in our English Bibles are *chronos* and *kairos*.

Generally speaking, *chronos* expresses the idea of a span or space of time. This could be "a moment of time" (Luke 4:5) or a "long time" (Luke 20:9). It can refer to "long ages past" (Romans 16:25) or more personally to "the time of your stay on earth" (I Peter 1:17). The main point isn't the length of time so much as it is the fact that a definite duration is being emphasized.

Kairos, on the other hand, is more concerned with the attributes of a given event or period than its extent. For instance, in Matthew 8:29 demons cried out, "Have You come here to torment us before the *kairos*?" They were complaining that their appointed time to face judgment had not yet arrived. Another example is Matthew 16:3, where Jesus chided the Pharisees because they could not "discern the signs of the *kairos;*" in other words, they were blind to the characteristics of the period of the Messiah as foretold by the prophets. He reiterated this in Luke 19:44 when He told them that they "did not recognize the *kairos* of [their] visitation."

Paul repeatedly used *kairos* to characterize the end times. In II Thessalonians 2 he said that the Antichrist will be revealed "in his *kairos*." In I Timothy 4:1 he wrote that "in later *kairos* some will fall away from the faith." In II Timothy 3:1 we are told that "in the last days difficult *kairos* will come." And then in the third verse of the following chapter "the *kairos* will come when they will not endure sound doctrine…" All of these instances are pointing out a particular feature of the end of the age.

Jesus' final words to His disciples hinted at the difference in these two terms: "It is not for you to know times (*chronos*) or epochs (*kairos*) which the Father has fixed by His own authority." (Acts 1:7) We could safely translate this statement to say: "It is not for you to know *time periods or their characteristics* which the Father has fixed by His own authority."

Vine's rightly sums up the difference in these two Greek terms: "*Chronos* marks quantity, *kairos*, quality."[7]

AN ETERNAL MINDSET

In spite of the fact that we live within the constraints of Time, we have been destined for another realm. As Solomon noted in Ecclesiastes, God has written eternity upon our hearts. He has set the reality of immortality within us; man has an unconscious awareness of the perpetual nature of life; indeed, it could be said that God has inscribed all the countless ages of the hereafter upon the human heart. That innate awareness is as real as a mother's instinct to care for her children, an animal's tendency to protect itself or a puppy's search for its mother's milk. An atheist must thoroughly deceive himself to arrive at the conclusion that there is no after-life. (However, I suspect the old adage is true: There are no atheists in a foxhole!)

In spite of the fact that the sense of eternity has been instilled within man's nature, he must still dwell within the confines of Time. A.W. Tozer captured man's challenge: "To be made for eternity and forced to dwell in time is for mankind a tragedy of huge proportions. All within us cries for life and permanence, and everything around us reminds us of mortality and change."[8]

Because man has been created for the eternal he‡ will find

---

‡ Throughout this book I regularly refer to people in the masculine form. This is not a slight against female readers. I just find that vacillating back and forth between the masculine and feminine forms or attempting to use a neutral term (e.g., they, them, their, etc.) makes for awkward writing and cumbersome reading.

that the temporal pleasures of this world will never offer real satisfaction. Indeed, isn't this the great message of the book of Ecclesiastes?

Solomon was given a free license to have everything earth life had to offer him. Ecclesiastes tells us that he filled his life with knowledge (1:16), pleasure (2:1), laughter (2:2), building projects (2:4-6), slaves (2:7), flocks and herds (2:7), silver, gold, and treasures (2:8), entertainment (2:8), and finally, sexual pleasure (2:9). In fact, he says, "all that my eyes desired I did not refuse them. I did not withhold my heart from any pleasure..." (2:10). Yet, before it was over, he had become a miserable and weary old man who "hated life" (2:17).

We see the same dissatisfaction in the lives of many modern Christians. The hectic pace of life and the inevitable stress that follows, the pursuit of position and status, and the unceasing indulgence in pleasure and entertainment combine to produce an earth-hugging life that cannot see beyond the great Now. It is certain to produce a despairing sense of meaninglessness because Temporal is stamped on all of it. Why does this make it feel so empty? Because man was created for another Time.

It reminds me of a scene I have witnessed on countless occasions driving on the back roads of Kentucky. There are occasions when the Western sky is lit up with a spectacular sunset. The panorama is made all the more striking when it is offset by a herd of cattle grazing on a bright green hillside in the foreground. How sad it is that those cows can't appreciate that beautiful scene. Not one single cow ever lifts her head to enjoy that beautiful sunset! The all-consuming desire for food keeps those cows completely engrossed in the small plot of earth and grass sitting in front of them.

Is it much different for modern man who becomes so enthralled with the scanty offerings of earth life? Like those grazing cows, most are content to spend their lives chewing on the bland diet offered by this temporal realm. If only we could live with the attitude of the psalmist. "O God enthroned in heaven, I lift my eyes to you," he exclaimed; "We look to Jehovah our God for his mercy and kindness just as a servant keeps his eyes upon his master or a slave girl watches her mistress for the slightest signal." (Psalm 123:1-2 LB)

WHERE IS THE HEART FOR HEAVEN?

If God has stamped eternity into the centermost part of our beings, why are we so taken up with "eating grass?" Why is it that we hardly give the magnificent sunset of heaven any more than a passing glance? Why aren't our lives more focused on the hereafter? After all, doesn't the Bible teach us that the heart sets the direction of our lives? (Proverbs 4:23) And if He has instilled the reality of eternity in our hearts, why don't we feel it compelling us onward and upward?

Charles Spurgeon encouraged the believers of his day along these lines when he wrote: "Christian, meditate much on heaven, it will help thee to press on, and to forget the toil of the way. This vale of tears is but the pathway to the better country: this world of woe is but the stepping-stone to a world of bliss. And, after death, what cometh? What wonder-world will open upon our astonished sight?"[9]

One would think that Christians would long to enter that land of joy, but by-and-large that doesn't seem to be the case. One example of this is the mentality prevalent in the Church that one should fight to preserve one's life at all cost. For instance, if a believer announces that he has been stricken with a life-threatening disease, the first reaction is an almost frantic sort of prayer—as if death is the worst imaginable thing that could happen to the person. Of course, the tendency toward self-preservation is inherent in all living beings. But shouldn't a longing for heaven set believers apart from the unsaved? Didn't Jesus say, "...he who hates his life in this world will keep it to life eternal."? (John 12:25) Where is the attitude Paul had when he wrote that he had "...the desire to depart and be with Christ, for that is very much better."? (Philippians 1:23) And doesn't Scripture promise us that Christ could "…deliver those who through fear of death have been living all their lives as slaves to constant dread."? (Hebrews 2:15 LB) I'm a firm believer in healing prayer and I know that there are occasions when it is God's will to restore life to a dying person. But it seems to me that there is something fundamentally wrong in the Christian who dreads death.

What a higher attitude Amy Carmichael exhibited. Elisabeth Elliot's excellent biography on Amy's life (*A Chance to Die*) offers an interesting anecdote that says much about Amy's attitude regarding death. One day an acquaintance told Amy that her doctor had diagnosed her with a heart condition and warned her that any sudden movement—such as quickly getting out of a chair—could be fatal. Amy's response was classic: "How do you resist the temptation to jump out of the chair?"

God has given man the capacity to long for heaven and to live with an eternal mindset, but that doesn't necessarily mean man will do so. We have been given a free will and we may choose to partake of or disregard this higher life.

Any believer who has spent much time reading his Bible instinctively knows that the kingdom of God is constantly beckoning his attention. But alas, the typical Christian lives such a harried existence that he simply doesn't take the time to quietly contemplate such vital truths. His or her life is more likely to be taken up with online networking, playing video games, watching television, rushing the kids to soccer practice, reviewing the sports scores or going shopping than considering these great issues. A terrible atrophy has settled into the spiritual lives of most believers. A soul-deadening lethargy has largely silenced such eternal matters for most.

Jesus Christ said, "So don't worry and don't keep saying, 'What shall we eat, what shall we drink or what shall we wear?! That is what pagans are always looking for; your Heavenly

Father knows that you need them all. Set your heart on the kingdom and his goodness, and all these things will come to you as a matter of course." (Matthew 6:31-33 PHP)

The apostle Paul reinforced this sentiment when he told his readers to "set your sights on the rich treasures and joys of heaven where [Jesus] sits beside God in the place of honor and power. Let heaven fill your thoughts; don't spend your time worrying about things down here." (Colossians 3:1-2 LB)

When we consider these biblical mandates in light of having a temporal versus eternal mindset, they take on new significance. Perhaps we could rephrase these statements to say: "Stop thinking like a dumb beast that can't see beyond what's in front of him. Lift up the eyes of your heart and take in the dazzling Celestial City that beckons you! Live your life with heaven as the great focal point and pursuit of the rest of your time on earth!"

When we think about it, isn't having an eternal mindset one of the things that sets believers apart from the godless culture in which they live? As one paraphrase interpreted the words of Jesus: "It's obvious, isn't it? The place where your treasure is, is the place you will most want to be, and end up being." (Matthew 6:21 MSG)[§]

---

§ It is with good reason that *The Message* paraphrase is controversial. While in some instances it can be helpful and enlightening, on other occasions it lacks Biblical accuracy. I quote it sparingly.

"This is what happens to those who live for the moment, who only look out for themselves: Death herds them like sheep straight to hell."
—The Psalmist[1]

"The wise man looks ahead. The fool attempts to fool himself and won't face facts."
—Solomon[2]

LIVING FOR NOW

W hile man has the capacity to live with a clear sight of the eternal, history tells us that most people will live out their lives with an overwhelming concern about the temporal.

One Christian in the Bible who exemplified this attitude is Demas—one of the apostle Paul's hand-chosen protégés who helped him while he was in prison. When Paul wrote Timothy his final epistle he had to tell Timothy that Demas, "having loved this present age, has deserted me…" (II Timothy 4:10)

Although Paul's short remark to Timothy was regarding his sadness over the loss of a dear one, it offers insight into the term "present." The Greek word translated "present" in this verse is *nun*, which is usually translated into English as "now." Here are a few examples of this Greek term:

- "Blessed are you who hunger *now*…" (Luke 6:21)
- "*Now* is the Son of Man glorified…" (John 13:31)
- "*Now* is the day of salvation…" II Corinthians 6:2)

When considering the temporal aspect of earth life, it

wouldn't be a stretch at all to translate "this present age" as the Now Age. Let's face it, Demas gave up the fight and sank down into the spiritual carelessness of his generation. Jesus could have been speaking about him when He said such a person has "no firm root in himself, but is only temporary, and when affliction or persecution arises because of the word, immediately he falls away." (Matthew 13:21) Another fitting assessment of Demas could have been this statement Jesus made: "For whoever is bent on saving his [*temporal*] life [*his comfort and security here*] shall lose it [*eternal life*]..." (Matthew 16:25 Amp)

The truth is that, by his actions, Demas chose to identify himself with his generation rather than God's kingdom. In stark contrast to Moses, he chose "the temporary pleasure of sin," rather than to "suffer affliction along with the people of God." (Hebrews 11:25 Dar) He gave himself over to living for the pleasures, comforts and temporal safety of this present age.

It is true that being associated with the apostle Paul was dangerous business. One never knew when the volatile Nero would suddenly launch a campaign of terror against Christians. There was always the possibility of a Roman soldier showing up at Paul's jail cell and executing him and everyone with him.

Perhaps Demas was with Paul when he wrote his first epistle to Timothy. Apostasy was clearly on Paul's mind when he penned that epistle. He spoke of those who had "denied the faith" (I Timothy 5:8), "wandered away from the faith" (I Timothy 6:10), "suffered shipwreck in regard to their faith" (I Timothy 1:19) and those who would "fall away from the faith." (I Timothy 4:1) Be that as it may, the sad story of Demas illustrates the live-for-now mindset of the people of this world and those who abandon Christ to return to it. There are a number of ways this thinking manifests itself.

THE IMPATIENCE OF EARTH LIFE

The godless people of this world are led in their choices through life by the dictates of their fallen natures. Those desires can range from the seemingly harmless (such as buying a car) all the way to indulging in flagrant sin. The real issue at stake isn't so much the level of sin one might be involved in as much as it is the mindset that he can live his life without concern about God's will. The thoughts and actions of such people are driven by a motivation to please themselves rather than God. With temporal pleasure as their main priority, they have no interest in enduring the trials involved in a true Christian life. Nothing will blind a person to the realities of the spiritual realm and the hereafter like sin and rebellion.

Of course, such people don't realize that they are being led along a godless course by spiritual enemies. (Ephesians 2:2) And the more they indulge those carnal passions, the greater the hold the enemy will have on their lives. Addictions are an extreme example of this spiritual dynamic, but it actually plays itself out in a thousand different ways in the typical person's life. Whatever the object of their lust might be, a sense of agitation will tend to grow in the person's heart until he gets what he wants.

This mindset is developed astonishingly early in life. One can often witness this lust in action in the toy section of a department store. Consider the young mother who is escorting her five-year-old through the store when, suddenly, the little tike spots a toy he wants. "Mommy," he says pleadingly, "I want that toy."

"Well, you can't have it, Johnny," she responds kindly.

"But mommy, I want it," he says, unable to grasp what seems to him to be an unfair denial of a perfectly reasonable request.

"You can't have everything you want, son," she patiently explains.

This explanation is unacceptable to the lust-driven little boy, however. One can feel the determination rise within him. He refuses to be denied what he wants. Of course, every parent understands that this is a battle of wills. Like a good parent, she holds her ground, knowing all too well that if she caves in to his demand, she will be hard pressed to win the next challenge.* The situation escalates and within minutes, the little kid is red-faced, lying on the floor, thrashing around, screaming for all he's worth.

We smile with compassion at the poor woman's dilemma, and yet, isn't this attitude buried in the heart of every human? Although most adults have learned to control themselves, occasionally we have all witnessed a grown-up throwing a childish tantrum. It is only the internal work of the Holy Spirit that can give a believer a decisive victory over such an immature attitude.

There have always been demanding people who become angry when they don't get their way. "They want what they want and they want it now," as the saying goes. However, this sense of inner agitation has flourished like never before in the prosperous and fast-paced lifestyle of 21st Century America. One need look no further than modern technology to see this. A few years ago Internet users were thrilled to be able to download content at speeds of one million bits per second. Today's Internet providers feel pressured by consumers to offer speeds one hundred times that fast. In my book, *Intoxicated with Babylon: The Seduction of God's People in the Last Days*, I described this phenomenon as a sign that we are living in the last days:

> Certainly, our post-modern world can accurately be described with the word motion. We are living in a time of unprecedented activity. People are rushing, people are moving, people are "on the go," living their lives in ceaseless locomotion. Stand on any bustling street corner and witness the stress that is etched into people's faces. Lean over a freeway overpass and watch the endless rush of speeding cars, often driven by

---

* "The rod and reproof give wisdom, but a child who gets his own way brings shame to his mother," says Solomon. (Proverbs 29:15)

frustrated and even angry drivers. Park near an airport and observe the crowded planes bound for multiple worldwide destinations. Truly, the whole world is in a full-court press. Of course, this was foretold in Scripture as one of the overriding characteristics of the end times: "many shall run (Heb. *shut*: rushing around) to and fro, and knowledge shall be increased." (Daniel 12:4 KJV)

Americans have become, dare I say it, addicted to this fast-paced lifestyle. Indeed, television programming experts now say that in order to hold a viewer's attention, the scene must change on the screen *every three seconds*, or they will become bored and change the channel! How much more will this be the case as entranced young video-gamers become the driving force behind modern society?

One of the unfortunate effects of such frenetic living has been a high level of impatience in people's lives. Our daily decisions are affected, much more than most of us realize, by how quickly we can accomplish a given task. Ray Kroc was the first to capitalize on this new phenomenon when he opened a chain of "fast food" restaurants named McDonald's™. The enormous success he enjoyed certainly did not come from the quality of the food he offered but from the fact that he could provide it instantly—*without waiting*. In our frenzied tempo of life, we want what we want NOW![3]

SPIRITUAL SHORTSIGHTEDNESS

In spite of the slow-paced lifestyle of biblical times, Scripture actually has quite a bit to say about those who are living for "now."

The biblical term "fool" perfectly describes a person who

routinely chooses the temporal over the eternal. I suppose the most telling characteristic of a foolish person is that he lacks the ability (and/or desire) to think through the consequences of his actions. Peter spoke of the man who "...is blind, [*spiritually*] shortsighted, seeing only what is near to him..." (II Peter 1:9 Amp) Solomon wrote, "The wise are cautious and avoid danger; fools plunge ahead with reckless confidence." (Proverbs 14:16 NLT) When it comes right down to it, foolish people just don't consider the long-term results of their actions. They impulsively respond to their emotions or desires with little regard to biblical instruction.

There was a time in my life that the word "fool" would have perfectly described me. I was terribly addicted to sexual sin. It was methodically destroying my life. I lived with a constant sense of shame and guilt, which, in turn, gutted me of self-confidence. My actions destroyed one marriage and nearly another. I wanted to live the life of a Christian, but my secret sin ruined every attempt to make my life right with God. And, needless to say, if I didn't repent of my sinful lifestyle I was going to end up in hell. Yet when some delicious temptation presented itself, none of this hindered me. I could only see the pleasure available to me at that moment. The long-term consequences of my actions seemed insignificant to me right then. Surely I was the classic fool.

Solomon could have easily been writing about the loose women I pursued when he wrote, "For the lips of an immoral woman are as sweet as honey, and her mouth is smoother than oil. But *in the end* she is as bitter as poison, as dangerous as a double-edged sword." (Proverbs 5:3-4 NLT)

This kind of folly isn't limited to sexual sin, of course. A tour of Skid Row will reveal many lives that at one time were full of promise and bright hope. Indeed, alcoholism has destroyed many people who once had successful careers. "Do not gulp down the wine..." said Solomon. "*In the end* it will bite like a snake and sting like a cobra." (Proverbs 23:31-32 NEB)

It would be wrong to think that shortsightedness is limited to those with addictions, however. For instance, how many people have destroyed everything decent in their lives because of an obsession to become wealthy? Who can forget the picture of Ebenezer Scrooge, whose insane greed had driven off the woman he loved and left him a miserable old man? "Money made hurriedly at the start turns out unblessed *at the end*," Scripture tells us. (Proverbs 20:21 Mof)

All three of these cases—and many others that could be mentioned—have one thing in common: those involved were headed for disaster. There is a Hebraic term which is italacized in each of the passages quoted above. It is the word *aharit*. The word means "the end of the matter" and is typically used to describe how a person's life ends up spiritually. Solomon's observation sums up the thinking of all such people: "There is a way which seems right to a man, but *its end (aharit)* is the way of death." (Proverbs 14:12)

The following two paraphrases bring out a little more fully the significance of this verse:

- There's a way of life that looks harmless enough; look again—it leads straight to hell. (MSG)
- Before every man there lies a wide and pleasant road that seems right but ends in death. (LB)

The foolish person cannot see the *aharit*; he can only see the "wide and pleasant road" that lies before him. He "...is blind, [*spiritually*] shortsighted, seeing only what is near to him..." (II Peter 1:9 Amp)

TEMPORAL SECURITY

Closely akin to the greedy man is the person who is obsessed with financial security. The actions of these two men are very similar, but their motives are slightly different. The Scrooge-type miser is a man who loves money for money's sake. He enjoys what it can do for him, especially the way he can lavish himself with whatever he desires. The person who has an inordinate desire to become financially independent tends to be more of a fretter who lives in fear of monetary ruin. His mood shifts up and down with the stock market indexes.

Even believers are prone to this mindset. Paul told Timothy, "Impress on those who are rich in the present (Gk. *nun*) age that they must not be haughty nor set their hopes on riches— that unstable foundation—but on God who provides us richly with all things for our enjoyment." (I Timothy 6:17 WNT)

One day Jesus also addressed this issue. He told His listeners, "Beware, and be on your guard against every form of greed; for not even when one has an abundance does his life consist of his possessions." (Luke 12:15) He then went on to illustrate this truth with a story about a rich farmer who had amassed so much wealth that he had to build new barns to contain it all. The Now-minded businessman said to himself, "Lucky man! You have all the good things you need for many years. Take life easy, eat, drink, and enjoy yourself!" (Luke 12:19 GNB)

This man's prosperity is very similar to that which most of us Americans enjoy. Of course, being wealthy in itself is not sinful. The problem comes when people attempt to find security, significance or fulfillment in their possessions and financial holdings. How many Christians are just as guilty of this kind of thinking as the unsaved?

The truth is that the more a person has of this world, the greater the hold those possessions tend to have on his heart. Not only are temporal riches unsatisfying, but they have the power to deplete the soul of the eternal riches God offers. Those with temporal wealth are usually consumed with concerns such as protecting themselves from losing their possessions, minimizing their tax load, finding new ways to luxuries and so on. The list of concerns grows in proportion to the wealth. As Alexander MacLaren put it: "The mad race after wealth, which is the sin of this luxurious, greedy, commercial age, is the consequence of a lie—that life does consist in the abundance of possessions."[4]

But, as we shall see even more vividly in the following chapters, sinners have no guarantees they will have a tomorrow to enjoy their riches. While the farmer Jesus spoke of gloated over his self-made life, the Almighty's voice boomed from heaven: "You fool! This very night you will have to give up your life; then who will get all these things you have kept for yourself?" (Luke 12:20 GNB)

That very night this man crossed into the terrifying realm of the hereafter, where the very demons who had nurtured and fueled his lust for money now awaited him. In spite of this man's extensive financial holdings, one thing is certain: he took none of them with him. In the end, the very thing that had promised him security was that which cost him his soul.

"And Jesus concluded, 'This is how it is with those who pile up riches for themselves but are not rich in God's sight.'" (Luke 12:21 GNB)

THE GREAT REJECTION

Ultimately, the issue with the ungodly is not so much about their shortsightedness, nor their lust for the pleasures of this temporal life; the real problem lies in their relationship to their Maker. It is the unbelief of the rebel who will not bow his knee to the Lord. "The impious fool says in his heart, 'There is no God.'" (Psalm 14:1 NEB) He doesn't want to believe in God because he doesn't want to be told what to do.[†]

One such fool was William Ernest Henley (1849-1903). He was an Englishman who was struck down with tuberculosis

---

† In numerous instances in the Bible, unbelief is manifested by rebellion to God's authority. Hebrews 3:18-19 is one such example: "And to whom did He swear that they would not enter His rest, but to those who were disobedient? So we see that they were not able to enter because of unbelief."

of the bone at the age of twelve. He suffered terribly with his malady and at the age of 25 his left leg was amputated below the knee. In spite of excruciating pain, he managed to complete college and carve out a literary career.

While he lay in a hospital bed in 1874, he penned a poem that revealed the anger and defiance smoldering inside him toward God. The title means "unconquered" in Latin.

INVICTUS

Out of the night that covers me,
Black as the Pit from pole to pole,
I thank whatever gods may be
For my unconquerable soul.

In the fell clutch of circumstance
I have not winced nor cried aloud.
Under the bludgeonings of chance
My head is bloody, but unbowed.

Beyond this place of wrath and tears
Looms but the Horror of the shade,
And yet the menace of the years
Finds, and shall find, me unafraid.

It matters not how strait the gate,
How charged with punishments the scroll.
I am the master of my fate:
I am the captain of my soul.

A discerning believer will quickly see the cynicism, despair and spiritual rebellion in some of his phrases. Although his bloodied head remained "unbowed," and he saw himself as the "captain of [his own] soul," he had a vague sense that one day he would face "the Horror of the shade."

Invictus is a fitting epitaph for all such rebels who prefer Satan's mantra: "It is better to reign in hell, than to serve in heaven."[5]

John Wesley describes the end of all such people:

> In what condition will such a spirit be after the sentence is executed, "Depart, ye cursed, into everlasting fire, prepared for the devil and his angels!" Suppose him to be just now plunged into "the lake of fire burning with brimstone," where "they have no rest, day or night, but the smoke of their torment ascendeth up forever and ever." Forever and ever! Why, if we were only to be chained down one day, yea, one hour, in a lake of fire, how amazingly long would one day or one hour appear! But after thousands of thousands, he has but just tasted of his bitter cup! After millions, it will be no nearer the end than it was the moment it began! How foolish of a man, who deliberately prefers temporal things to eternal.[6]

And so it is that those who live for the moment will one day be forced to face the terrible reality of the great realm of eternity. Such is the terrible plight of the godless generation in which we live.

*"A generation comes and a generation goes,
but the earth remains the same through the ages."*
—The Preacher[1]

*"Show yourselves guileless and above reproach,
faultless children of God in a warped and crooked generation,
in which you shine like stars in a dark world"*
—The Apostle Paul[2]

A POSSESSED GENERATION

One of the ways God measures time is through the unfolding of the human race. In fact, Moses defined Genesis—the book of beginnings—as "the book of the generations of Adam." (Genesis 5:1) He then devoted the rest of that chapter to laying out the genealogical line from Adam to Noah.

Biblically speaking, the term "generation" typically refers to a group of people alive during a particular period, in relation to their line of ancestors. A generation was commonly considered to be around forty years—the typical length of time between a man's birth and his maturity.*

Living conditions didn't change much from one generation to the next during biblical times—except under extraordinary circumstances, such as a particularly wicked or godly king coming to power. For the most part, the way people lived their lives continued on in the same vein over hundreds of years. There are a couple of different reasons for this.

---

* It should be noted that there is one occasion when a generation is said to be one hundred years. (Compare Genesis 15:13 and 15:16.) Modern generations are considered to be between 25-30 years—the average length of time between *the birth of parents and that of their offspring.*

For one thing, in those days the biggest influence on a child's life was his parents. Little girls wanted to grow up to be just like their mothers and little boys tended to see their fathers as their heroes. Thus, children usually lived their lives in the same manner as their parents. This is no longer the case. The primary influencers in the lives of most kids today are either older kids or teenage media stars. Some pastors (especially in homeschooler communities) are so concerned about the power of peer pressure that they do not offer youth groups in their churches; the kids remain with their parents during services.

Another reason that our culture is changing from generation to generation is that we live in an era of rapid technological advance. For example, when I was a teenager we didn't have the Internet—with all of the evil influences available on it; we didn't communicate with each other by emails or text messages; we didn't have cell phones. Relationships were much more personal back in the Sixties.

Our culture has undergone tremendous upheaval in the past century. In fact, life is so different from one generation to the next that we now assign names to each. In the past hundred years we have seen the "Lost Generation" (who lived and fought during WWI), the "Interbellum Generation (who lived during the 20's and 30's), the "Greatest Generation" (who lived and fought during WWII), the "Baby Boomers" (born in the post-war years), the "X Generation" (c. 1965-1983), the "Y Generation" (born in the '80s and '90s) and so on.

Many generations have come and gone since the dawn of man. To one degree or another, each has had its own personality, formed by the age and culture in which it has existed. Indeed, the term is often used to describe a class of people within a certain culture that are characterized by some common disposition: a "righteous generation" or a "perverse generation."

There are three periods of time in biblical history that strike me as times when the contrast between light and darkness stood out most intensely. Each of these ages is characterized by their distinct cultures.

AN UNPREPARED GENERATION

The first body of individuals we will examine were those who escaped slavery in Egypt. Regarding this generation, the Lord said, "For forty years I was continually disgusted with that generation, and I said, 'These people desire to go astray; they do not obey my commands.'" (Psalm 95:10 NET) They were also called "a warped and crooked generation" (Deuteronomy 32:5 NIV), "a mutinous generation" (Deuteronomy 32:20 NEB), "a stubborn, twisted generation" (Deuteronomy 32:5 LB), "a self-willed race" (Deuteronomy 32:20 Mof) and "a stiff-necked and uncontrolled generation; a generation whose heart was hard, whose spirit was not true to God." (Psalm 78:8 BBE) What did these people do to provoke such harsh terms from biblical writers?

Ingratitude and unbelief were the most prominent characteristics of this generation. To understand what Moses faced on the desert of the Sinai, we must take a quick perusal of their history.

The descendents of Jacob lived and flourished in Egypt over a four-century span. This entire period is hardly mentioned in Scripture. I suspect what happened to God's people during that epoch was a source of great pain to Him. The fact is they had walked right into an ancient culture teeming with fertility cults and dark wisdom. Over time, this spiritual darkness overtook them and entrenched itself within the Jewish community. The Lord had no choice but to ordain circumstances in such a way that the Egyptians turned against the Jews. Before it was over with, they were languishing in cruel servitude. They weren't looking for spiritual deliverance; they only cried out to the Lord because of their slavery. They would have gladly remained in their idolatry had they not been forced to endure such harsh treatment.

Over time, the lash of the Egyptian whip provoked within the Jewish community a great cry for deliverance from the God of their forefathers. At just the right time, God raised up, prepared and sent them a man named Moses.

The story is well known. The proud pharaoh refused to release his nation of slaves. Jehovah pummeled the Egyptians with plague after plague until he relented. The mightiest nation on earth was crushed by the God of the Jews.

Unfortunately, being segregated from the evil influences of Egyptian culture and its gross idolatry did not change the corporate mindset of the Hebrews. They longed for the carnal indulgences of the fertility cults. They had little interest in the higher life being offered by God. Time and again they criticized Moses and murmured against the Lord. Yet Jehovah showed great patience toward them, again and again overlooking the rebellious attitude that had entrenched itself in that generation. His last great effort at winning their hearts—by showing them the Promised Land—only gave them another opportunity to turn against Him. In spite of all of the miraculous events they had witnessed, they refused to believe He could overcome the nations that occupied Canaan. When they rejected the testimony offered by Joshua and Caleb, God made the decision to let that generation die out in the wilderness. He would begin the Jewish nation in the Promised Land with their children. Surely it was "...a stubborn and rebellious generation, a generation that did not prepare its heart and whose spirit was not faithful to God." (Psalm 78:8)

WHEN THE FOUNDATIONS ARE SHAKEN

The second corporate body of Jews I wish to highlight is that group living during the reign of King Saul.

After Moses died, Joshua led the next generation to conquer and possess the Promised Land. The destruction and capture of Jericho began an exciting new period for the young nation.

One city-kingdom after another fell before Joshua's advancing army. Gradually the Twelve Tribes took possession of their respective areas.

> The people served the Lord all the days of Joshua, and all the days of the elders who survived Joshua, who had seen all the great work of the Lord which He had done for Israel. Then Joshua the son of Nun, the servant of the Lord, died at the age of one hundred and ten...
>
> All that generation also were gathered to their fathers; and there arose another generation after them who did not know the Lord, nor yet the work which He had done for Israel. Then the sons of Israel did evil in the sight of the Lord and served the Baals, and they forsook the Lord, the God of their fathers, who had brought them out of the land of Egypt, and followed other gods... (Judges 2:7-12)

Once again, a new generation ushered in a different ethos. For the most part, the Jewish people languished in self-will and idolatry during the next three centuries. Spiritual darkness became so prevalent during that period that "word from the Lord was rare in those days." (I Samuel 3:1)

It was then that the Lord raised up Samuel, to counteract this horrible spiritual decline. For perhaps twenty years Samuel did his utmost to lead his generation into a true worship of Jehovah. Finally, after being mercilessly oppressed by the Philistines, the Israelites responded to his pleas and "removed the Baals and the Ashtaroth and served the Lord alone." (I Samuel 7:4) It was the highpoint of Samuel's long career as a prophet and judge. The Israelites—now empowered by God—dealt a crushing defeat to the Philistines, thus ending forty years of oppression.

Eventually their commitment to Jehovah waned once

again and the pagan-enamored people began complaining to Samuel that they wanted to be led by a king rather than by the theocratic form of government he oversaw.

As is so often the case, God gave the people what they demanded: an impressive looking young man named Saul. For the next forty years (one generation), Saul reigned as a cruel dictator, spiritually running the country right into the ground.

In the meantime, God was working in the life of a young man named David. As an attendant to the king, he was privy to the wickedness of Saul's dynasty. One day, one of his friends lamented to him, "The foundations of law and order have collapsed. What can the righteous do?" (Psalm 11:3 NLT)

Yes, it is true, Psalms 11 and 12 tell of a time when society on the whole had turned bad. The friend of young David who uttered the words above had certainly rightly discerned "the spirit of the age" in which he lived. A heavy blanket of evil seemed to rest upon the land. "The god of lies [had become] enthroned in the national heart."[3] There was an acute shortage of godly men. Society seemed to have reached the last stage of corruption "when vileness is exalted" and "the wicked strut about on every side." (Psalm 12:8)

No wonder David's timid friend complained. "No matter how hard we try to live godly lives," he probably whined, "the world around us only gets darker. It's hopeless to fight this losing battle! What can a righteous man do but bend to such times?"

Of course, David did continue to fight the fight, and when Saul's miserable life was finally extinguished, he was installed as the king of Israel. His inauguration ushered in the "Greatest Generation" the nation of Israel ever produced.

A PERVERSE GENERATION

After David's death, the nation of Israel once again relapsed into its old ways. One corrupt king after another led the people down the dark path of sin and idolatry. Eventually, the northern tribes were exiled to Assyria and Judah was taken captive into Babylon.

Something evil was broken in the Jewish nation during the Babylonian exile. The infatuation with idolatry which had plagued the Jewish nation from its inception was rooted out. Unfortunately, the clearing away of that corporate evil only served to open the door for another type.

It began following the Maccabean revolt against the Syrian leaders during the Second Century B.C. The Pharisee party was birthed as an answer to centuries of worldliness. In fact, the word "Pharisee" actually means, "separatists," from the Hebrew word, *parash*, "to separate." They emerged from the numerous religious and political sects prevalent during this period to become Judaism's most prominent "denomination."

By the time Jesus arrived on the scene in the First Century, a cold formalism had become entrenched in Judaism. That generation of Jews became known more for maintaining a religious façade than for sincere devotion to the Lord. Jesus hit the nail squarely on the head when He said, "But they do all their deeds to be noticed by men; for they broaden their phylacteries, and lengthen the tassels of their garments." (Matthew 23:5) Everything involved in their ceremonial exercises—whether it was wearing phylacteries or reciting long prayers in public—was done for the purpose of making themselves appear to be spiritual to those around them.

Jesus' appearance was like a fresh wind in the stale air of religiosity. He immediately captivated the hearts of the Judean people, drawing multitudes to Himself by His miraculous deeds and deep spirituality. The Pharisees watched all of this unfold with cautious interest and suspicion.

Within a year or so of His ministry beginning, the Pharisees had become openly hostile to Jesus. It came to a boiling point when Jesus cast a demon out of a blind and mute man. (see Matthew 12) Some of the people began suggesting the possibility that He really was the long-awaited Messiah. This infuriated the

Pharisees and, under a dark inspiration, they accused Him of being demon possessed and acting as a direct representative of Satan. His miraculous power was irrefutable—and since they could not acknowledge that it came by the hand of God—it could only mean that Jesus was empowered by Satan.

In response to this blasphemous accusation, Jesus appealed to their logic by asking questions of His own. "If Satan casts out Satan, he is divided against himself; how then will his kingdom stand? Or how can anyone enter the strong man's house and carry off his property, unless he first binds the strong man?" (Matthew 12:26) He then went on to warn them about blasphemy: attributing to Satan the works of the Holy Spirit.

While in the midst of this discussion, one of them rudely interrupted Him. "Teacher, we want to see a sign from You." It was an insincere demand for proof of His claims.

"It is a wicked, godless generation that asks for a sign; and the only sign that will be given it is the sign of the prophet Jonah..." He responded. He then went on to give them a chilling prediction. "At the Judgment, when this generation is on trial, the men of Nineveh will appear against it and ensure its condemnation, for they repented at the preaching of Jonah; and what is here is greater than Jonah." (Matthew 12:39-41 NEB)

After mentioning the spiritual hunger of the Queen of Sheba as another source of condemnation to them, He took an interesting twist in His line of reasoning:

> When an unclean spirit comes out of a man it wanders over the deserts seeking a resting-place, and finds none. Then it says, "I will go back to the home I left." So it returns and finds the house unoccupied, swept clean, and tidy. Off it goes and collects seven other spirits more wicked than itself, and they all come in and settle down; and in the end the man's plight is worse than before. That is how it will be with this wicked generation. (Matthew 12:43-45 NEB)

This was a very profound revelation. Not only did it give insight into the way demons operate regarding individual lives, but it also revealed how they can function within an entire generation.

The Jewish nation of the First Century was certainly not involved in the kinds of gross idolatry and wickedness of past generations. No, this was a new and perhaps more virulent form of evil: it was the utter giving over to self-righteousness of nearly an entire nation. In essence, the unspoken attitude conveyed by the Jewish leaders was that they had no need of God's righteousness; they had their own. (Romans 10:3)

Yes, the principalities that had taken root within Israel through idolatry had been expelled through the national repentance that had occurred during their exile in Babylon. Never again would the open worship of demonic images be a significant problem amongst the Jewish people. The evil intruders had indeed been expelled from the house of Israel. It was "unoccupied, swept clean, and tidy." But the national repentance did not last. The superficial reformation that occurred only left a vacuum: one which was soon filled by a new breed of spiritual squatters.

The ugly self-righteousness that became entrenched in the Jewish culture was so contrary to God's heart that it drove the people to murder the Messiah Himself. The old demons associated with the fertility cults were replaced by seven new ones: hypocrisy, superciliousness, nationalism, disdain for others, greed, a critical spirit and, of course, self-righteousness. Thus, their plight was even "worse than before."

The great sin of the First Century Jews was that they were given Light—like no generation had ever received—and they rejected it. Once they, as a people, had concluded that Jesus was a fraudulent Messiah, there was nothing left to do but to murder Him. Surely the demonic spirits came back with a sevenfold vengeance. No wonder Jesus called them an "evil generation."

For us, the more relevant lesson to be learned through the words of Jesus is that it is possible for demonic spirits to possess an entire culture.

Of course, we find this spiritual phenomenon hinted at elsewhere in Scripture. When Daniel was praying for his people during the Babylonian exile, an angel told him that he had attempted to respond sooner to his prayers but that "the prince of the kingdom of Persia" had withstood him. (Daniel 10:13) Certainly this must indicate a powerful entity had, in some inexplicable way, inhabited a nation of people.

And of course, one can only imagine what Paul had witnessed in the unseen realm for him to express what he did in Ephesians 6:12. Some of the terms he used regarding Satan's army were so profound and enigmatic, that I will once again turn to various paraphrases to bring out the magnitude of what he wrote in that verse. He called them:

- the world rulers of this present darkness (AMP)
- cosmic powers of this dark age (GNB)
- the potentates of the dark present (Mof)
- all the various Powers of Evil that hold sway in the Darkness around us (TCNT)
- those who have mastery of the world in these dark days, with malign influences in an order higher than ours (Knox)
- the empires, the forces that control and govern this dark world—the spiritual hosts of evil arrayed against us in the heavenly warfare (WNT)
- organizations…the unseen power that controls this dark world, and spiritual agents from the very headquarters of evil (PHP)
- the evil rulers of the unseen world, those mighty satanic beings and great evil princes of darkness who rule this world; and against huge numbers of wicked spirits in the spirit world (LB)

It seems apparent to me that Scripture is revealing the possibility of an entire people group to be dominated and controlled by powerful, satanic beings. When the enemy forces can become so entrenched within a culture that they are able to control its corporate mindset, surely it must be a possessed generation.[†]

We might well ask ourselves how the Lord would characterize our current Christian generation. What does He see when He scans the American Church? Do you think He would characterize us as a godly generation? Or do you think He would find it difficult to distinguish us from the culture in which we live?

Whatever the case may be, we all will be required to give an accounting of our lives—whether we lived in a time when godliness reigned or whether we lived in the midst of a perverse generation. The times in which we live surely affect us all, but ultimately each of us will either respond or reject the Lord's authority. This will prove to be the great question regarding the way we used our time on earth.

---

† This helps to explain why the Lord would order the extermination of an entire race of people such as the Amalekites. (I Samuel 15:3)

"They who go down to the pit cannot hope for Your
faithfulness...their probation is at an end, their destiny is sealed."
—Isaiah[1]

"Life is the time of probation, and while it lasts
the vilest of the vile is within the reach of mercy.
It is only in eternity that the state is irreversibly fixed, and
where that which was guilty must be guilty still."
—Adam Clarke[2]

ON PROBATION

Time, of course, is merely an intangible measurement of our existence upon Earth. The important question is not, What is time? The question that demands an answer is, What is the purpose of it and what we will do with the time that has been allotted to us?

Life on earth is probationary in nature. The purpose of our time here is that we might decide once and for all if we want to be a part of (and subject to the laws of) God's kingdom or if we would prefer to remain detached from that realm and live for ourselves. God has given us His Word to show us the way into salvation. He has sent His Son to die on the Cross so that we might have that salvation. If people show by their neglect or outright rejection of this provision that they do not care to be a part of His kingdom, their eternal doom does not prove that God is unmerciful.

Every human has been allotted a short probationary period on this earth. All of the trials and temptations of life are meant to bring to light what is within the heart. Earth is where the mettle of our character is tested; where we are afforded the opportunity to help the widows and orphans in their distress, to free the imprisoned and to warn the perishing. In other words, we have this one chance to do something worthwhile, something which will follow us into the hereafter.

These opportunities are over once our time on earth has ended. As Jesus said, "We must work the works of Him who sent Me as long as it is day; night is coming when no one can work." (John 9:4)

At this point it is still possible for you and me to obey God, live out His love to those around us, to resist temptation and do our utmost to please Him. But before we know it, the curtain of life will fall, the sun will set and our earthly scenes will come to an end. The door of opportunity will be closed, and we will never again pass this way. Our character will be fixed, our destiny will be sealed and eternity will be upon us. When it's all said and done, what will we have to show for our time on earth?

MAN'S LIFESPAN

Earth life seems so long, but it actually flies by amazingly quickly. David fully understood this. "You, indeed, have made my days short in length," he wrote; "and my life span as nothing in Your sight. Yes, every mortal man is only a vapor." (Psalm 39:5 Hol)

Every human being has been allocated a certain timeframe on earth. Job acknowledged this to the Lord, "Mortals have a limited life span. You've already decided how long we'll live— you set the boundary and no one can cross it." (Job 14:5 MSG) Solomon wrote, "Man's steps are ordained by the Lord…" (Proverbs 20:24) And Jesus clearly alluded to this when He asked, "And which of you by worrying can add a single hour to his life's span?" (Luke 12:25)

One way to illustrate a person's duration on earth is to hold up a pencil in the midst of a great auditorium. That pencil represents a person's entire 70 or 80-year lifespan. One can look at that short pencil in comparison to the vastness of the assembly hall and get a small sense of how our time on earth pales in light of the immensity of eternity.

A significant term in the Old Testament, "day" (Heb. *yom*), is used nearly 2,000 times. The consequence of this word can be sensed in some phrases that come up repeatedly in Scripture: "length of days," "days prolonged," "days are complete," "all the days of his life," "full of days" and so on.

The illustration below can help us get a sense of what our lives look like from God's vantage point. The dots that form the line could represent the days a person has been appointed.* The asterisk to the far right represents a person's final day on earth.

✿✿*

From God's eternal perspective, He sees each and every human being plodding along his timeline. The Psalmist wrote, "The Eternal looks from heaven, beholding all mankind; from where he sits, he scans all who inhabit the world." (Psalm 33:13-14 Mof) The lives of every living being are "laid bare to the eyes of Him with whom we have to do." (Hebrews 4:13)

Not only does He see individuals, but He can also see Time in its entirety. "For a thousand years in Your sight are like yesterday when it passes by, or as a watch in the night." (Psalm 90:4) This explains why God can foretell events of the future.

Scripture makes it clear that God has allocated a certain amount of time for every human being. Job queried, "Is there not an appointed time to man upon earth?" (Job 7:1 KJV) Solomon said, "No man has...authority over the day of death." (Ecclesiastes 8:8)

The seeming predictability of death can cause us to forget that God really does hold a person's life in His hands. The monotonous repetition of life and death makes it seem as though people live and die completely at the mercy of Nature. The truth is there are countless doors into eternity. Consider the

---

* A 70-year life would be over 25,000 days; obviously a page in a book doesn't afford us the room to lay that number of dots out!

unexpected deaths of some of the following famous people:

Jack Daniels, the notorious whiskey distiller, found his way into eternity by throwing a temper tantrum. He showed up at his office one morning in 1911 and kicked his floor safe when he couldn't remember the combination to it. An infection set up in his big toe which brought about his early demise. His final words offer insight into the eternity awaiting him: "One last drink, please."

Harry Houdini, who found fame by continually cheating death, finally met his fate when a man challenged his boast that he could take any blow to his body above the waist without injury. The man hit him several times, not knowing that he was already suffering from appendicitis. The famous magician died several days later from peritonitis when his appendix ruptured.

Another man who lived a daring life was General George Patton. After leading his men on a number of heroic campaigns in World War II, he unexpectedly died a few months after the war ended. He and another general were riding in the back of a Jeep on their way to hunt pheasants in postwar Germany when a military truck pulled out in front of the Jeep. It was only a minor collision, but it was enough to cause the old warrior to hit his head on a metal bar in the vehicle. He died less than two weeks later from pulmonary embolism.

Then there is the case of martial arts actor Bruce Lee. He was 32-years-old and in his prime when he dropped dead of cerebral edema after taking a common pain killer called Equagesic. He apparently died because of a hypersensitivity to the muscle relaxer found in the drug. The coroner ruled it "death by misadventure."

Interestingly, his 28-year-old son Brandon died twenty years later in a freak accident while filming the movie *The Crow*. He was shot in the spine with a prop gun that inexplicably had a live round in the chamber.

In addition to these, there are the cases of actor Vic

Morrow who walked into a helicopter propeller during filming of *Twilight Zone: The Movie* and author Tennessee Williams who choked to death on an eye-drop bottle cap. These incidents are only a handful of the countless "freak accidents" that bring about premature deaths throughout the world every day. The reverse case makes the same point. The following three accounts are of young girls who were the sole survivors of airline disasters.

In 1971, a turboprop plane with 92 people on board crashed in the Amazon rainforest. Juliane Koepcke, age 17, was strapped into a row of seats that somehow landed in a tree. Suffering from a concussion and a broken collarbone, she endured a ten-day walk through crocodile and piranha infested rivers to reach safety.

In 1993, nine-year-old Erika Delgado was aboard a DC-9 that crashed near Bogota, Colombia. She apparently survived the plunge when she landed on a mound of seaweed. She later claimed that God told her to stay right where she was and, sure enough, a farmer soon came to her rescue.

Francesca Lewis, 13, was aboard a Cessna plane with four other people that crashed in a mountainous area of Panama in 2007. She was found by rescuers two days later pinned upside down in her seat suffering from hypothermia and a broken arm. A pile of luggage that had fallen on top of her protected her from the elements.

These three youths—along with countless other people down through the ages—were spared certain deaths by the merciful intervention of Providence. One would wonder what God's purpose was in extending their lives. Is it possible the Lord was giving each of them a new appreciation for the brevity of life? Could it be that they were not prepared to face eternity? And especially regarding adults who have avoided untimely deaths—were they being afforded another opportunity to do something positive with their lives?

THE DAYS OF THE RIGHTEOUS

Life is fragile at best, but it is of the utmost comfort to believers that theirs are carefully watched over and guarded by the Almighty. He is personally and intricately involved in the lives of His people. David said, "The Lord knows the days of the blameless..." (Psalm 37:18) Think of that! God knows about every single dot on your timeline. He is intimately familiar with every 24-hour period you will experience during your stay on earth. He knows what each day will bring—as you move down your timeline. David went on to add: "The Lord directs the steps of the godly. He delights in every detail of their lives." (Psalm 37:23 NLT)

The sweet psalmist of Israel seemed to grasp God's involvement in his life better than any other biblical character. When he reviewed the Lord's past dealings with him, all he could see was mercy. And when he scanned the horizon of his future with his eyes of faith, he found that he had no reason to believe anything would be different. His faith was firmly planted upon the goodness of God's character.

This confidence in the Lord would certainly explain why he was able to courageously face death throughout his life. And perhaps it explains why he could confidently write, "Surely goodness and mercy shall follow me all the days of my life; and I will dwell in the house of the Lord forever." (Psalm 23:6 NKJV) In his mind, he could see "goodness and mercy" sitting at each dot on his timeline, awaiting his arrival. And once his time on earth was complete, he saw an eternity that would be spent "in the house of the Lord."

Maybe it was clearer to David than most of us, but every true believer can certainly share the same testimony of God's mercies. Our lives, our timelines, are held securely in His trustworthy hands. Surely this should offer great comfort to all of us!

The truth is that God chose for you to live at this exact time in the history of mankind. Our births did not come about by some genetic accident. The Preacher said that God "sets the time for birth and the time for death..." (Ecclesiastes 3:2 GNB) Surely this is true of those who were chosen "in Him before the foundation of the world." (Ephesians 1:4) In every sense of the word, this is *our time.* In some inexplicable way we were created to be part of the end-times Church.

The apostle Paul warned believers that the last days would be "perilous times of great stress and trouble [*hard to deal with and hard to bear*]." (II Timothy 3:1 Amp) This peril is primarily spiritual: we live in a time when many will fall away from the living God.

Yet it is also a time of unprecedented opportunity for sincere believers. There has never been a period in Church history when believers can so easily study the Word of God, have access to such rich worship music, regularly hear so many great preachers and even minister to countless people in need. Surely we could join with the disciples in saying, "Blessed are the eyes which see the things which we see, and hear the things which we hear!"

And it needs to be said that, regardless of the great physical dangers present in our day, our lives will not last one day longer or be ended one day shorter than God has ordained. As someone once said, Christians are immortal until their life's work has been completed. There is no guarantee that our journey will be an easy one, but at least we know it is in God's hands.

> *"Plagues and deaths around me fly,*
> *Till he please I cannot die*
> *Not a single shaft can hit*
> *Till the God of love sees fit."*

Be that as it may, like all mortal beings, we too will eventually come to the asterisk at the end of the line of dots. But what a glorious blessing to us that we can face that day with bright hope and calm dignity! "To die is gain," for true believers. We have been freed of the fear of death that once had a grim hold upon us. Why would any Christian fear it? We have nothing to look forward to but everlasting joy and happiness!

THE FEARFUL FUTURE OF THE UNSAVED

Believers can look tomorrow in the face without flinching, but this is not the case for those who remain outside of God's will. Rebels who play fast and loose with this life are taking a fearful chance every time they step out their front door. Each day presents new perils to their souls. Consider what is expressed in Psalm 37 alone about the danger the unsaved face:

- They will "wither quickly like the grass and fade like the green herb" (vs. 2)
- They "will be cut off" (vs. 9)
- "Yet a little while and the wicked man will be no more" (vs. 10)
- "You will look carefully for his place and he will not be there" (vs. 10)
- "Their sword will enter their own heart" (vs. 15)
- They will "perish" and "like smoke they vanish away" (vs. 20)
- They are "cursed" and "cut off" (vs. 22)
- Also, their descendents "will be cut off" (vs. 28)
- The righteous will see the wicked cut off (vs. 34)
- They will "pass away" and "not be found" (vs. 36)
- They will be "altogether destroyed" and their posterity will be cut off. (vs. 38)

All of these biblical statements are variously stating the same basic truth: death is but a breath away for an unbeliever. The Angel of Death stands over the person with drawn sword, awaiting word that the person has crossed the line of no return, that it is time for him to face Judgment.

Verses 12 and 13 are especially revealing: "The wicked plots against the righteous and gnashes at him with his teeth. The Lord laughs at him, for He sees his day is coming." In other words, the Almighty is constantly aware of the end of that person's life. His days are numbered and the Lord is ever mindful of the asterisk on his timeline. The time is quickly approaching when He will bring "their days to an end in futility and their years in sudden terror." (Psalm 78:33)[†]

It is interesting how unconcerned the typical unbeliever is about his eternal destiny. He seems to live under a strange illusion that somehow everything will work out in his favor in the end. He can offer no facts to support this buoyant perspective, yet he firmly holds onto it nonetheless. But alas, when it is all said and done, "he has let the appointed time [*in which God had him on probation*] pass by!" (Jeremiah 46:17 Amp)

An amazing story about Jonathan Edwards[‡] perfectly illustrates how blind a person can be to his eternal danger. One day, a neighbor showed up at the renowned minister's door seeking his advice. It seems that the man, well-known for his alcoholism, had had a frightening dream the night before. In it, he had died and been sentenced to hell, but at the last moment, was granted a reprieve under the stipulation that if he did not reform his ways within one year, his pardon would be revoked. He woke from his dream drenched in sweat at the terrible realities of that world of doom.

---

† While there is nothing the godless can do to assure themselves of a long life, it could certainly be argued that they have the capability to shorten it through reckless living or even suicide. Likewise, the case of Hezekiah (II Kings 20) argues for the possibility of the Lord extending the life of a righteous person. Perhaps this two-fold truth is what Solomon was referring to when he wrote, "Fearing the Lord prolongs life, but the life span of the wicked will be shortened." (Proverbs 10:27 NET)

‡ Jonathan Edwards is famous for the sermon, "Sinners in the Hands of an Angry God." He later became the president of Princeton University.

Jonathan Edwards heard the man out before offering his thoughts. "This is a solemn warning from God to your soul," the revivalist said. "You must give heed to it and forsake your sins, or you are a ruined man for eternity." The terrified man proclaimed himself a changed man, swearing that he would never again return to the bottle. After his neighbor left his home, Edwards noted the incident in his personal journal.

The sobered man proved true to his word. For several months he gave up drink and faithfully attended church. However, over time, he began missing meetings and eventually threw off all pretense and returned to his old ways. One night, while completely intoxicated, he walked out the back entrance of his favorite saloon. As he started down the stairwell, he tripped, fell headlong down the stairs and broke his neck. Pastor Edwards heard about it the next day and, upon checking his journal, discovered that his death happened one year to the day after his alarming dream.[3]

This story is truly a fitting example of the probationary nature of earth life. Who can say but that Providence has granted every one of us at least one such extension of life? The fact is we humans are on this earth to test the mettle of our hearts. None of us are guaranteed tomorrow.

*"Seek the Lord while He may be found;
call upon Him while He is near.*
—Isaiah[1]

*"The time of Jesus is kairos—a time of opportunity.
To embrace the opportunity means salvation;
to neglect it, disaster. There is no third course."*
—John Marsh[2]

TODAY IS THE DAY

One of the great rules that govern the spiritual realm is the law of opportunity. Along the road of life's journey, the typical unbeliever will arrive at certain junctures where the Holy Spirit will convict him about his need for salvation. It is a *kairos*: a divinely appointed occasion where a person is offered the chance to enter the kingdom of heaven.

These occasions are not as haphazard as they may seem. A person's lifetime may appear to be a chaotic jumble of isolated and disjointed events. To what degree the life of an unbeliever is actually under the direct control of God is debatable. However, what is undeniable is that those certain eternal moments when the Lord draws near to a person are not a result of happenstance.

Truth be known, the Holy Spirit has worked behind the scenes in the lives of most of these people for many years: arranging circumstances, creating crises or bringing them into the acquaintance of believers. God loves people and "desires all men to be saved and to come to the knowledge of the truth." (I Timothy 2:4) How tirelessly He works to bring people into His kingdom!*

---

* The prayers of believers provide the main catalyst in this process.

Considering the amount of effort the Lord puts into saving a person's soul, it is certainly understandable why the apostle Paul warned people about "resisting," "quenching" and even "grieving" the Holy Spirit. It is dangerous business to bite the hand that is offering life and hope and salvation.

One apt example of this is found in the story of the apostle Paul and Felix, the governor of Palestine. (Acts 24) The two had talked a number of times, but one day the aged minister saw an opportunity presenting itself to win the Roman procurator to the Lord. It came about in a completely unforeseeable way when Drusilla, Felix's Jewish wife, asked to hear about "The Way."

For his part, Felix was at least open to hearing the gospel message. No doubt Drusilla had told him some of the ancient tales about the great Yahweh of Israel. It is even possible that Cornelius—that godly centurion assigned there in Caesarea—had shared the gospel with him at some point.

Whatever the case may be, Paul took advantage of this opportunity to earnestly tell the governor about Judgment. The aged apostle spoke with confidence, passion and authority. Felix grew increasingly uncomfortable. Paul's words seemed to unleash a strange power within his heart. Felix found himself trembling as the pressure to make a decision for Christ mounted.

In spite of the fact that the governor was visibly shaken, he still resisted. For a Roman politician to join a disdained off-shoot of Judaism would not only make him a laughingstock of his Roman cohorts, but it would immediately ruin his political aspirations. He felt torn between a sense of spiritual urgency and the dread of the consequences that would surely follow. It was then that he was inspired with a way to relieve the pressure he was experiencing.

"While Paul was discussing righteousness, self-control, and the coming judgment, Felix became frightened and said, 'Go away for now, and when I have an opportunity (Gk. *kairos*), I will send for you.'" (Acts 24:25 NET) The crisis was over. He, like so many others in similar situations, mistakenly believed he could choose his own *kairos*. (see also John 6:44)

As a prisoner, Paul was in no position to argue. However, if he could have, he might have said something along these lines: "Now is the acceptable time, and this very day is the day of salvation. (II Corinthians 6:2 PHP) Don't you see, most excellent Felix? This is your *kairos*—perhaps the one great opportunity you will ever have to make your life right with God. For you today—now—the kingdom of heaven is at hand! Don't squander this precious, eternal moment! You have no guarantee you will have another chance like this again!"

Spiritual procrastinators have every intention of responding to the message of the gospel. They are convinced it is the right thing to do; they just don't want to do it *today*. They imagine that they can force Time to work on their own schedule. They entertain some vague notion that it will be easier to do the right thing at some point in the future.

"I always have tomorrow," they assure themselves. But it would be wise for them to consider the words of James: "How do you know what will happen even tomorrow? What, after all, is your life? It is like a puff of smoke visible for a little while and then dissolving into thin air." (James 4:14 PHP)

One of life's great deceptions is that tomorrow will be the same as today. The very mundane nature of life seems to confirm its changelessness. One day seems to roll into the next in one long, weary blur.

There are two primary problems with putting off until tomorrow the salvation being offered today. First, there is no guarantee there will be a tomorrow. If there is one thing certain about our stay on earth it is that a person's entire life can be changed—or even cut down—in an instant.

Secondly, even if life outwardly remains the same from day to day, an imperceptible inner transformation occurs over time. Little by little the heart grows colder to the things of God. Life in a fallen world has a way of gradually changing even the nicest person into someone who will eventually become incapable of responding to the Lord.

Kairos experiences only serve to heighten the stakes. The person will either have a marvelous spiritual breakthrough or their rejection of God's offer will hasten and deepen the hardening process occurring within. The person may only mean to delay his answer to the divine summons, but even inaction is a response. Each time a person ignores such an appeal, the heart grows increasingly more calloused. A person's character is forged by such experiences.

The truth is that the hardening of the human heart is the culmination of years of satanic deception and self-delusion. Eventually, the day of reckoning must come, as Albert Barnes so eloquently describes:

> That danger [of delusion] deepens every day and every hour. If it is continued but a little longer it will be broken in upon by the sad realities of death, judgment, and hell. But then it will be too late. The soul will be lost—deluded in the world of probation; sensible of the truth only in the world of despair…
>
> Soon he will be at the judgment bar, and from that high and awful place look on the past and the future, and see things as they are. But, alas, it will be too late then to repair the errors of a life; and amidst the realities of those scenes, all that he may be able to do, will be to sigh unavailingly that he suffered himself to be deluded, deceived, and destroyed in the only world of probation, by the trifles and baubles which the great deceiver placed before him to beguile him of heaven, and to lead him down to hell![3]

SHEER NEGLECT

While procrastinators understand their lost condition and just can't seem to "pull the trigger" on making a commitment to the Lord, there is another type of person whose situation is even more dangerous. I'm referring to the pseudo-Christian who imagines he belongs to the family of God when he really doesn't.†

He is very open about his affiliation with the evangelical movement. He attends a Bible-preaching church; understands and believes orthodox Christian doctrine; and is very familiar with Christian lingo, prominent preachers and church ethics. His lifestyle gives every indication that he is a committed believer.

However, if those around him could see beneath the surface, they would discover that he is actually very careless about his spiritual life. There is a limit to his commitment to Christ. Although he knows his way around Christian circles, his relationship to God amounts to little more than superficial head knowledge. He has never really taken the time to comprehend the true meaning of the Cross nor allowed the Truth to penetrate his heart; in short, he has never been converted. He is every bit as unsubmitted and unsurrendered to Christ as Felix was. He is more culpable because salvation is something that sits neglected right under his nose.

Crises, such as the one Felix experienced, ineffectually glide over him because he has just enough religion to make him feel confident about his eternal destiny. This false sense of security nullifies the Holy Spirit's every attempt to reach him.

It was to just such people that Paul asked the startling question: "How shall we escape if we refuse to pay proper attention to the salvation that is offered us today? How will we escape if we neglect so great a salvation?" (Hebrews 2:3 PHP)‡

The Bible consistently presents man's salvation as something of tremendous value. And yet, if the pseudo-Christian were honest with himself, he would not be able to say that he considered it "great." If he truly believed it was, he would treat it as the precious thing that it is. (see Matthew 13:44-46)

---

† Those who have grown up in Christian homes are often the most susceptible to this delusion.

‡ Most Bible scholars believe Paul wrote the book of Hebrews.

Since a relationship with God means so little to him, he is mostly unmindful of it. Like the sluggard of Proverbs 24 who wouldn't tend to his garden, he has allowed the spiritual life available to him to be overrun with weeds.

This man is a spiritual laggard. His lackadaisical approach to the gospel has not produced a true salvation. Jesus said, "Strive to enter through the narrow door; for many, I tell you, will seek to enter and will not be able." (Luke 13:24) Other translations bring out the urgency even more clearly:

- Strain every nerve to force your way in through the narrow gate (WNT)
- You must do your utmost to get in through the narrow door (PHP)
- Be endeavoring with a strenuous zeal to enter through the narrow door (Wuest)
- Exert every effort to enter through the narrow door (NET)
- Agonize to enter in through the narrow gate (GDBY)
- The way to life—to God!—is vigorous and requires your total attention (MSG)

That great revivalist Charles Finney shares the fearful results of such neglect:

> Do not presume upon God's forbearance. You think God is too good to cut you down in your sins;— but you may find He is too good to spare you—too good to let you allure others down to hell—too good to let you accumulate more guilt, and make your eternal doom more dreadful. It is the worst of all folly to neglect this great salvation because you know that God is merciful. Mere neglect secures the soul's ruin...The day of hope is gone, and their neglect has proved fatal.[4]

Oh, how a glimpse out of the realm of Time would change such a flippant attitude! Consider what would happen to the neglecter if he could spend but a moment on the outer fringes of hell: if he could smell the stench of sulfur and burning flesh, sense the despair of outer darkness, catch a glimpse of the lake of fire or hear the screams of its inhabitants. Perhaps then he wouldn't treat such a great salvation with such contempt.

Just as powerful would be the effect of spending a moment in heaven. What if he could smell the aroma of celestial flowers, sense the overwhelming atmosphere of joy, take a quick look at the streets of gold or hear the happy chatter of the redeemed. Maybe that would bring about an improved attitude about the salvation he takes for granted.

THE FINAL CALL

God loves people and is typically willing to wait a long time for a sinner to repent. Even the vilest offender still has hope so long as he has breath in his lungs. He still remains within the grasp of divine mercy.

Eventually however, the person crosses a line of no return and God initiates actions to bring about his demise. (Genesis 15:16; Matthew 23:32) At this point—and completely unknown to him—the books are closed and his fate has already been settled. Perhaps it is some final act of defiance that seals his doom. This will often come as one final offer of divine clemency.

One such situation presented itself to a godly Methodist who lived and ministered in the South about a century ago.

This particular Sunday morning, he felt a strong compulsion to preach on Proverbs 29:1: "A man who hardens his neck after much reproof will suddenly be broken beyond remedy."

He arrived at the church that morning to discover, to his amazement, a local doctor—known for his wicked lifestyle and his open cynicism of Christianity—sitting in the congregation. Unbeknownst to this sinful man, his time on earth was running out. In fact, "in less than two hours he would be millions of miles away in a distant world, lost and forever undone."[5]

The service continued along normal lines for the first 45 minutes: opening prayer, announcements, an offering and several hymns. The malefactor impatiently endured all of this.

By the time the minister took his position behind the pulpit, the doctor's probationary period on earth was down to a mere hour. The pastor preached his heart out that morning about the terrible judgment rebels were certain to face. He spoke with a fire from above—a message so compelling that one would expect it to bring any transgressor to his knees.

Instead of softening the physician's heart, the sermon only seemed to provoke a greater determination within him to resist it. At first, looks of impatience, boredom or even skepticism would occasionally cross his face. But before long, a sneering grin filled the offender's face.

The pastor had never encountered such a brazen display of insolence in all his years of ministry. He was becoming increasingly unnerved by the man's defiance. By the time he started to conclude the message, he felt he was looking right into the face of the devil himself; the man's eyes filled with darkness and contempt.

The infidel was definitely getting the better of this battle of wits, but he was doing so to his own destruction. The man of God finally concluded his sermon and sat down, leaving the scoffer to gloat over his victory.

It was to be short-lived. Little did he know that he had less than ten minutes left to his life on earth. Ten minutes! A vast, eternity of misery lay stretched out before him. He had but a few short moments to make amends for a lifetime of rebellion and wickedness. His one and only hope was that the Holy Spirit could somehow reach his conscience, but alas, it was a conscience that had been seared one too many times. "His death warrant and doom were read in his hearing and he did not know it. He crossed the Dead line and did not realize it.

The last warning had come, been delivered, tarried and gone; and he to whom it was sent, was oblivious of its arrival and ignorant of its departure."[6]

After the closing hymn, the pastor offered the final benediction. The parishioners were dismissed and went their different ways. The doctor arrogantly strutted out the door and mounted his horse.

The pastor was engaged in conversation with some parishioners when, not more than five minutes after the benediction, the loud crack of a gunshot reverberated in the air. This was immediately followed by the cries of a frantic man running into the church. "The doctor's been shot! He's dead!"

The minister and a few of the remaining church members rushed to the scene. "They found the physician's horse browsing on the grass, and close by, lying stone dead on the ground was the doctor with his face upturned to the sky, his black eyes wide open and staring aloft, as if he was watching the flight of his lost soul as it sped on its way to the Judgment Bar of that God whom he had resisted and grieved and insulted up to the last hour of his life."[7]

Some unknown assailant had hidden in a clump of bushes and shot the unwary physician right through the head.

Such are the perils of those who delay, neglect or reject the Holy Spirit's overtures. As we saw in the last chapter, none of us are guaranteed tomorrow. Aren't the eternal implications enough to cause us to reconsider the way we are living our lives on earth?

"Don't you realize that from the beginning of time,
ever since people were first placed on the earth,
the triumph of the wicked has been short lived and
the joy of the godless has been only temporary?"
—Zophar the Naamathite[1]

"You live in an age that is twisted out of its true pattern,
and among such people you shine out, beacons to the world."
—The Apostle Paul[2]

6

Emerging from the Earth Life

Any study on the subject of Time and Eternity would be incomplete without an examination of the word "age" (Gk. *aion*). It is a term biblical (and evangelical) writers have employed to mark out and describe various eras in man's history.

A quick scan of the centuries of Time reveals the great epochs marked out by God: the Antediluvian Age, the Age of the Patriarchs, and on down to our present Church Age. Even the hereafter was called by our Savior "the age to come." (Mark 10:30) It goes without saying that all of these eras are held in the hands of the great Eternal.

However, the term *aion* is often extended beyond that basic meaning to refer to an ungodly mindset that rules in the hearts of unredeemed man. It is the word which New Testament writers used to describe the "Live for Now" mindset which the spirit of this world constantly promotes among mankind.*

---

* *Aion* is very similar to the Greek word *kosmos* in that both are used to describe different aspects of the ungodly attitudes and perspectives of the world: *kosmos* describes its rebellious attitude toward God's authority while *aion* is used to convey its temporal way of viewing life.

Jesus talked about "the worries of the *aion*" (Mark 4:19), "the sons of this *aion*" (Luke 16:8) and "the end of the *aion*" (Matthew 13:39). Paul said, "The god of this *aion* has blinded the minds of the unbelieving" (II Corinthians 4:4). He also mentioned "the rulers of this *aion*" (I Corinthians 2:8), those who consider themselves to be "wise in this *aion*" (I Corinthians 3:18) and those who "are rich in this present *aion*" (I Timothy 6:17).

It is the spiritual significance of this term that draws our attention. In one sense, the fallen world in which we live has certain characteristics that are true no matter in what historic period a person finds himself. In his epistle to the Ephesians, Paul touched on the three common characteristics true to every age:

> "And you were dead in your trespasses and sins, in which you formerly walked according to the course (*aion*) of this world (*kosmos*), according to the prince of the power of the air, of the spirit that is now working in the sons of disobedience. Among them we too all formerly lived in the lusts of our flesh, indulging the desires of the flesh and of the mind, and were by nature children of wrath, even as the rest." (Ephesians 2:1-3)

Man's life is lived out within the confines of planet earth and the temporal realm it inhabits. This small passage of Scripture contains within it the entirety of man's dilemma. It can be summed up under the familiar headings: the world, the flesh and the devil. Let's examine these in light of the bigger picture of mankind's spiritual condition.

SPIRITUAL DEATH

It should go without saying that human beings have a fallen nature: "sons of disobedience," "dead in their sins," "indulging their carnal passions." One of the characteristics of the unredeemed is lawlessness. Earth life affords every human being the privilege to choose to obey God's commandments or to live in self-will. People have been given a free will and have the option to live for the temporal pleasures of this world if that is what they desire.

This is seen everywhere one looks. The godless live carefree lives, raising their families, enjoying all of the world's entertainment, perhaps taking excursions to Las Vegas or even indulging in illicit drugs and sex. The issue isn't the level of sin they are involved in, but the fact that they live for themselves with little or no thought about God. Thoughts of the hereafter are far from their thinking. They are living for Today.

This carefree existence of unbelievers does not go unnoticed by godly people either. Sometimes it can dishearten the stoutest saint. Asaph was one such person. He was appointed as worship leader by King David because of his great love for the Lord and his ability to lead others into His presence. And yet, Psalm 73 recounts the story of how he became discouraged one day and nearly got himself into real spiritual trouble. "My feet came close to stumbling," he later confessed, "my steps had almost slipped." Asaph nearly slid into a pit of depression and despair when he began to focus on "the prosperity of the wicked."

"They are not in trouble as other men," he lamented to himself, "nor are they plagued like mankind." Asaph could not reconcile the fact that "the wicked" seemed to be blessed, while life seemed to offer him nothing but trouble. "Surely in vain I have kept my heart pure and washed my hands in innocence; for I have been stricken all day long and chastened every morning."

Asaph's discouragement nearly set his feet on the slippery path of self-pity. With his attention focused on the prosperity of the evil men of his day, he began to question the goodness of God. One more precarious step in that direction could have been disastrous; but Asaph was a man who knew his God. "When I pondered to understand this, it was troublesome in my sight until I came into the sanctuary of God. Then I perceived their end. Surely You set them in slippery places; You cast them down to destruction. How they are destroyed in a moment! They are utterly swept away by sudden terrors!"

It's so easy for sincere believers to become discouraged when they see the prosperity of the ungodly. However, one need only fast forward to the unbeliever's last moments on earth. Lying there on his deathbed, earth life has nothing left to offer him. He has lived for pleasures he can no longer enjoy. His good times have abandoned him like disloyal friends, leaving him with nothing but a bed of misery and an uncertain future.

The unbeliever would be horrified if he could peer just beyond the veil of the Temporal to see what awaited him. Maybe he would see leering demons now anticipating his death like so many morbid vultures. Perhaps he would see the massive, black cavern of hell lying beneath him. Whatever the case may be, surely the godless man has nothing good awaiting him in eternity.

THE COURSE OF THIS WORLD

Yes, earth life affords people the opportunity to throw themselves into self-centered living. It is this mentality that all unredeemed mankind—with their varied conflicting interests and philosophies of life—holds in common.

Paul calls it the "course of this world," or, more properly, the "*aion* of this *kosmos*." Or, we could say, the live-for-now-temporal-mindset of this rebellious world. This mentality leads people to live for temporary pleasure and disregard the eternal implications of flouting God's authority. Translators were correct to call it a "course," because it is the common path of the entirety of unsaved humanity. Jesus called it "The Broad Way."

Indeed, comparing these two phrases (from Ephesians 2:2 and Matthew 7:13) offers a fascinating glimpse into the unseen realm of this world—especially as it is expressed in different translations:

- You were…under the sway of the tendency of this present age…(Ephesians 2:2 AMP)
- You drifted along on the stream of this world's ideas of living…(Ephesians 2:2 PHP)
- You followed the fashion of this world…(Ephesians 2:2 Knox)
- You ordered your behavior as dominated by the spirit of the age in this world system…(Ephesians 2:2 Wuest)
- The gate to hell is wide and the road that leads to it is easy, and there are many who travel it. (Matthew 7:13 GNB)
- The highway to hell is broad, and its gate is wide enough for all the multitudes who choose its easy way. (Matthew 7:13 LB)
- …that leads away to ruin and everlasting misery. And many there are who are constantly entering through it. (Matthew 7:13 Wuest)
- …great numbers go in by it. (Matthew 7:13 BBE)

However this path is communicated, it is the way of the world. It is the self-pleasing life of the masses. People don't need to be taught how to fit into this corporate mindset: they need only follow their natural inclinations. They don't go through life with the prayer on their lips, "Thy will be done"; their lives are summed up in the brazen attitude, "My will be done." It takes no effort to live in the mass stream of mankind heading down the Broad Way.

This rebellious mindset is part-and-parcel of the human race. Most people are oblivious that they are caught up in this evil world's mindset, or that there even is such a thing. It is so engrained in our culture that people are totally unaware that they are slowly, but surely, marching to their own destruction.

THE PRINCE OF THE POWER OF THE AIR

It is no haphazard fate that binds together mankind in their rebellion. There is a great rebel spirit lurking in the shadows goading men on toward eternal destruction. He is the audacious traitor who led the great insurrection in God's kingdom. "The devil and his angels" have infested our planet and led mankind into rebellion against the Lord's authority.

As we saw in Chapter Three, this dark kingdom is made up of "persons without bodies—the evil rulers of the unseen world, those mighty satanic beings and great evil princes of darkness who rule this world...huge numbers of wicked spirits in the spirit world." (Ephesians 6:12 LB)

Satan is not called the "god of this *aion*" (II Corinthians 4:4) because he possesses divine attributes, but because mankind pays him their homage. As Albert Barnes writes, "They obey his will; they execute his plans; they further his purposes, and they are his obedient subjects."[3] People have willingly joined in his mutiny because, in his realm, they are free to pursue and fulfill their base passions.

Earth truly is a dark planet. Mankind is entrenched in spiritual darkness and is unable to extricate itself. "The god of this *aion* has blinded the minds of the unbelieving." (II Corinthians 4:4) Elsewhere Paul explained man's spiritual dilemma even further: "Their minds are full of darkness; they wander far from the life God gives because they have closed their minds and hardened their hearts against him." (Ephesians 4:18 NLT) Martyn Lloyd-Jones offers the following commentary on these verses:

> A kind of pall has descended upon and is covering the minds of all people who are not Christian. The god of this world has blinded their minds. It is precisely another way of saying that their understandings have been darkened...

The highest faculty in man has become blunted
and blinded; he cannot see because of the pall that has
descended upon him; he is surrounded by darkness. The
most disastrous effect that the Fall of Man produced
upon man was in his understanding.[4]

TRANSFERENCE

People are held in the grip of the "world forces of darkness."
They trudge along the Broad Way to destruction, their minds
fully under the sway of "the prince of the power of the air."
Surely, left to himself, every human being is hopeless. But God
has not left us to ourselves. His desire is to rescue us from this
"earth life." And so from the foundation of the world, from
the time that man fell, He has had a plan in place to redeem
man and free him from the "course of this world" that we are
all subject to. The next statements the apostle Paul makes in
Ephesians 2 offer hope:

> But God's mercy is so abundant, and his love for
> us is so great, that while we were spiritually dead in our
> disobedience he brought us to life with Christ. It is by
> God's grace that you have been saved. In our union with
> Christ Jesus he raised us up with him to rule with him in
> the heavenly world. He did this to demonstrate for all time
> to come the extraordinary greatness of his grace in the
> love he showed us in Christ Jesus. (Ephesians 2:4-7 GNB)

This grand exhibition of God's grace toward His people
has two distinct purposes—both of which are implied in the
last sentence (Ephesians 2:7), depending upon how a person reads
Paul's statement. Both ways of understanding this statement
are undoubtedly true and are certainly magnificent!
Some people understand it to refer to how the Lord will
be unfolding different aspects of His grace to His people

throughout eternity. Wuest's translation of this verse brings out this version: "in order that He might exhibit for His own glory in the ages that will pile themselves one upon another in continuous succession, the surpassing wealth of His grace in kindness to us in Christ Jesus." What a tremendous thought to ponder! Age upon age will reveal new aspects of God's blessings upon His people!

The second way of looking at this statement would seem to indicate a larger purpose: the final vindication of God's character, i.e., the enormous amount of grace that God has bestowed upon repentant people. It will be something to marvel at for all eternity.

Let's face it, from time immemorial Satan has maligned the Lord's good name. It began in the Garden of Eden. With just three words, "Has God said...?", the devil initiated a long-term and systematic campaign to assassinate God's reputation. He went on to suggest that the Lord was withholding good from Eve, the underlying suggestion being that "God is not trustworthy; He's in it for Himself."

For 6,000 years, the Lord has *allowed* Satan to work his poisonous deception into the minds of mankind. He has maligned God's character—not just to man—but also to "the rulers and the authorities in the heavenly places." (Ephesians 3:10) God's righteousness must, and ultimately will, be vindicated.

The goodness of God's character will not be completely seen until the final curtain of earth life has been drawn. It will take place before the great Throne of the Almighty as multitudes of redeemed saints will be showcased as trophies to God's mercy and grace. Dr. Martyn Lloyd-Jones wrote the following about this great day:

> This is to me the most overwhelming thought that we can ever lay hold of, that the almighty, everlasting, eternal God is vindicating Himself and His holy nature and being, by something that He does in us and with

us and through us…He is going to put us on display, as it were; there is going to be a glorious exhibition. He is already doing it, but it is going to continue in the ages to come, and at the consummation God is going to open His last great exhibition and all these heavenly powers and principalities will be invited to attend. The curtain will be drawn back and God will say, Look at them! "To the intent that now unto the principalities and powers in heavenly *places* might be known by the church the manifold wisdom of God."[5]

Yes, Jesus Christ has purchased for Himself a people who will be His bride. Paul earnestly reminds us that "we must never forget that he rescued us from the power of darkness, and re-established us in the kingdom of his beloved Son, that is, in the kingdom of light." (Colossians 1:13 PHP)

And so it is that, through the glorious grace of God, the elect are empowered to emerge from Planet Earth with saving faith and a bright eternal future. Meanwhile, they must live within the confines of Time with all of its various implications.

*"Lord, I know that none of us
are in charge of our own destiny;
none of us have control
over our own life."*
—Jeremiah[1]

*"A thousand things
enter into God's calculation
which do not enter
into man's reckoning.
The clock of heaven does not
measure days and years;
it measures events
and necessities."*
—J.D. Davies[2]

Part Two:

LIVING IN SIMULTANEOUS WORLDS

*"We must strip off every handicap, strip off
sin with its clinging folds, to run our appointed
course with steadiness, our eyes fixed upon Jesus
as the pioneer and the perfection of faith..."*
—the book of Hebrews[1]

*"The man who can drive himself further
once the effort gets painful is the man who will win."*
—Sir Roger Bannister

A RACE WITH TIME

S cripture uses different metaphors to describe the
Christian life: a fruit tree, a vine branch, a narrow path,
a soldier's life, a pilgrimage and so on. Each one is used
to illustrate some particular aspect(s) of the believer's time on
earth.

One metaphor that was employed repeatedly by biblical
writers was that of the footrace, a sport made popular in the
ancient Greek Olympics. In his epistle to the Philippians, Paul
used it to illustrate the sometimes strenuous nature of the
maturing Christian life:

> "I don't mean to say I am perfect. I haven't learned
> all I should even yet, but I keep working toward that day
> when I will finally be all that Christ saved me for and wants
> me to be. No, dear brothers, I am still not all I should
> be, but I am bringing all my energies to bear on this one
> thing: Forgetting the past and looking forward to what lies
> ahead, I strain to reach the end of the race and receive the
> prize for which God is calling us up to heaven because of
> what Christ Jesus did for us." (Philippians 3:12-14 LB)

By the time Paul wrote this letter to the Philippian believers (c. 63 A.D.), he had worked his way through some twenty years of his own spiritual timeline. After all that he had experienced, all that he had accomplished for the kingdom of God and all that he had suffered, he was still fighting the good fight and striving toward the finish line. Within five years he would die a martyr's death.

I suppose it is the strenuous effort involved in a race that is its most telling feature. Eyes locked on the finish line, every muscle strained, the runner pushes himself to the limit of his strength to complete the race. It is a sport that requires great determination and tenacity.

Paul uses this metaphor to illustrate the process of spiritual growth that should go on in the life of a believer. Time is one of the necessary elements to a race, albeit in a different way than Paul used it. Obviously, the person who runs the course the fastest (in the least amount of time) is declared the winner.

Paul was making a different point, however. He did not use the concept of a race to illustrate speed but the effort and endurance that is required to complete the contest. These terms could certainly be used to describe the sanctification process a believer experiences over "the long run."

A person does not grow simply by responding to an altar call, reading a Bible passage, saying a prayer, heeding the words of a wise counselor, enduring a trial or receiving a divine impartation. All of these spiritual elements play an important role in the overall process, but it is as our wise heavenly Father implements them through the passage of time that they are effective in bringing about change. Someone quipped, "Time is how God keeps everything from happening all at once."*

While time certainly has its place in this important soul-altering work, it alone will accomplish nothing. A runner lazily meandering

---

* God knows what His children can handle and typically spreads out over time life's challenges. Job's ordeal is one of the few occasions when the Lord—for His own purposes—allowed everything to pile on the dear man all at once. There are those occasions when the old adage holds true: When it rains, it pours.

along the course, perhaps sitting down for a rest occasionally, would be an apt description of the uncommitted Christian who imagines that he is becoming godlier simply by the passage of time.

No, it requires great effort on the part of the believer. The Holy Spirit is the One who brings about the internal transformation of character, but this only occurs as the person cooperates with His efforts, "strip[s] off every handicap, strip[s] off sin with its clinging folds," and does his utmost, for his part, to live the life of a true Christian. This process does take time, of course; but it is "time well spent" that accomplishes the work.

Actually, the very word used in Hebrews 12:1 to describe a "race" is the Greek word *agon*. It is a term which is closely associated with strenuous, painful activity. In fact, it is the word from which our English word *agony* is derived. The Vine's Bible dictionary brings out the fuller sense of these concepts: "(a) 'to contend' in the public games...(b) 'to fight, engage in conflict...' to strive as in a contest for a prize, straining every nerve to attain to the object...'the inward conflict of the soul.'"[2]

In light of that definition, consider some of the different ways *agon* is used elsewhere:

- *Strive* to enter through the narrow door; for many, I tell you, will seek to enter and will not be able. (Luke 13:24)
- Everyone who *competes* in the games exercises self-control in all things. (I Corinthians 9:25)
- Experiencing the same *conflict* which you saw in me, and now hear to be in me. (Philippians 1:30)
- For I want you to know how great a *struggle* I have on your behalf...(Colossians 2:1)
- I have *fought* the good *fight*, I have finished the course, I have kept the faith. (II Timothy 4:7)

The level of effort involved on the believer's part in the maturing process stands out clearly when considering these passages. Yes, it is a race, but it is one which must be run with an enormous amount of personal effort. As Alexander MacLaren put it, "Every foot of advance has to be fought; it is not merely 'running,' it is conflict as well... The runner...must tax muscle and lungs to the utmost, if, panting, he is to reach the goal and win the prize."[3]

THE GOAL

In the passage in Philippians quoted above, Paul brings out some other important elements that deserve attention.

Once the runner steps onto the track, his eyes are fixed on one object: the finish line. There is a goal to be accomplished, a mountain to be conquered, a contest to win, a race to complete. It is the finish line—and the victor's crown—that supply the motivation required to exert the enormous amount of effort that will be required.

The Hebrews 12 passage provided at the beginning of this chapter states it very clearly when it says we "run our appointed course with steadiness, our eyes fixed upon Jesus as the pioneer and the perfection of faith..." Indeed, to "consider Jesus" is one of the primary challenges of the entire book of Hebrews.

Yet, in our Philippian passage, Paul seems to contradict the idea of Jesus being the goal of the race. He infers that becoming "perfect" is the great goal of the race: "I don't mean to say I am perfect (Gk. *teleioo*)...but I keep working toward that day when I will finally be all that Christ...wants me to be."

So which is it? Is Christ Himself our goal or is it the maturity of the believer's life? Well, it's both, of course. This apparent contradiction is cleared up when we consider the Greek term: *teleioo*. It means "to accomplish, complete, consummate, fulfill, or make perfect." To help bring out its real meaning, consider four of its other usages in Scripture.

- Therefore you are to be *perfect*, as your heavenly Father is *perfect*. (Matthew 5:48)

- We proclaim [Christ], admonishing every man and teaching every man with all wisdom, so that we may present every man *complete* in Christ. (Colossians 1:28)
- Therefore leaving the elementary teaching about the Christ, let us press on to *maturity*...(Hebrews 6:1)
- Consider it all joy, my brethren, when you encounter various trials, knowing that the testing of your faith produces endurance. And let endurance have *its perfect* result, that you may be *perfect* and complete, lacking in nothing. (James 1:2-4)

All four of these passages of Scripture express different aspects of the same thing: maturing spiritually and becoming more like Christ. It doesn't mean that God expects us to be some kind of spot-free replica of His Son; He only requires us to sincerely and earnestly strive toward that higher life.

What a comfort to know that Jesus, "the hope of glory," is the *teleios* for every believer. One of the primary secrets to Paul's endurance in the great spiritual battle he fought over the years was that he was able to keep his eyes fixed on his dear Savior. Yes, the finish line was Christlikeness and all that that would mean in the hereafter. But just as important to him was seeing His beloved Savior standing at the end of the race cheering him on. So, as you can see, we set our eyes upon Jesus, the One whom we wish to emulate.

FORGETTING THE PAST

Unquestionably, the memory is one of the most important mental functions our Creator has provided to humans. Asaph said, "I shall remember the deeds of the Lord; surely I will remember Your wonders of old. I will meditate on all Your work and muse on Your deeds." (Psalm 77:11-12) It is through the contemplation of how God has treated us in the past that we acquire confidence to face the future. It is by considering the miracles He has previously performed in our lives that we have faith for the miracle we need today. What a rich heritage has been built into us! And just think of it: the timeline of God's past dealings with us has been inscribed into our minds. Surely it is true, "The memory of the righteous is blessed." (Proverbs 10:7)

Paul certainly knew the value of remembering the past. By the time he wrote his letter to the Philippians, he had witnessed God's work in his life in many ways. His introduction to Christianity was nothing less than a vision of the Messiah on the Damascus road. After a number of years of preparation, God used him to establish churches all over the regions of Galatia, Pisidia and Asia. God also used this one man to establish a beachhead for the gospel in the dark continent of Europe—right there at Philippi. Over those years, he had enjoyed enormous success in ministry and had undergone an extensive array of spiritual experiences, including being taken up into the third heaven.

Surely he didn't go through life avoiding any thoughts of the past. In fact, at one point in his second letter to the Corinthians, he recounted all the various ways he had suffered for the cause of Christ. (II Corinthians 11:23-29) And how many times did he share his testimony to kings, governors, Jewish leaders, church groups and passersby in the street?

So what could he have been referring to when he instructs us to forget the past? The aged apostle is clearly telling his readers that using their memories in an unhealthy way will stunt their spiritual growth.

I can think of several types of people who fit this mold. Have you ever known anyone who constantly talks about "the way it used to be?" To hear them tell it, the only time God has ever done anything significant was in the past, when they were young. They seem to be completely out of touch with what the Lord is doing in the present and they don't seem to be too concerned about what He might do in the future. All they want to talk about is "the good old days."

Then there are those who seem to gain their spiritual worth from past accomplishments rather than maintaining an ongoing trust in the Lord for their salvation. Perhaps this is partially what Paul was referring to earlier in Philippians 3. After citing all his achievements as a "righteous Jew," he said, "...I have put aside all else, counting it worth less than nothing, in order that I can have Christ, and become one with him, no longer counting on being saved by being good enough or by obeying God's laws, but by trusting Christ to save me..." (Philippians 3:8-9 LB)

Another person who constantly looks backward is the one who cannot let go of the sins and failures of the past—to the point of being debilitated by them. Some people seem to be unable to detach themselves from "the sins of their youth." They recount over and over the many times they failed God, offended other people or committed embarrassing deeds. In a strange way, they almost seem to relish focusing on past mistakes. How will they ever move into all that God has for them in the days ahead if they are forever walking backwards?

Of course, there are times we need to consider the sins we have committed. But the simple act of repentance allows us to walk away from those mistakes and leave them behind us. A person who focuses too much on past failures will only discourage himself. It is much healthier to look our mistakes "squarely in the face," learn from them, commit ourselves to a new course of conduct and then go forward with a renewed commitment to do better.

Someone said that failure is not falling down; it is remaining there when you have fallen. A scene from the movie *Chariots of Fire* is a perfect example of this. In one of Eric Liddell's early races, one of the other racers inadvertently tripped him. Many people would have sat there on the track sulking. But Eric had a champion's heart. Without hesitation he jumped up, took off running and actually won that race!

It is true that there are aspects of the past that are a blessing to recall, but there are other memories that are better left buried in the past!

LOOKING FORWARD

There is one aspect to failure that can actually be a help if used in the proper way: the awareness of our own shortcomings. The person who is satisfied with his current spiritual status might as well go sit in the grandstands and watch the real athletes perform. He is unfit to be included in the contest.

Possessing a healthy discontentment with oneself is one of the characteristics found in every great man or woman of God. The Lord does not chide His children for their faults and usually not even for occasional transgressions; what He will not allow to go on unchecked is a lackadaisical attitude about the work He desires to do inside of them.

Sad to say, but some Christians hardly give any thought to the lack of Christlikeness exhibited in their lives. Ungodly attitudes fester in their souls, habitual sins remain undealt with and intact, selfishness and pride flourish within them. How can they run the race and fight the fight with all of this baggage weighing them down? All of this is of little concern to such people: "For in his own eyes he flatters himself too much to detect or hate his sin." (Psalm 36:2 NIV)

We cannot back our way into heaven; we must, like all sprinters, stretch forward with all our might across the finish line. We must fight, struggle and strive all the way through the course God has laid out before us. And we will do all of it "in the strength of his might."

Paul said, "I am bringing all my energies to bear on this one thing..." There is something to being single-minded about the Christian life that compels the person ever onward. The double-minded man is unstable in all of his ways. He cannot focus on the finish line because his faith is like "like the surf of the sea, driven and tossed by the wind." (James 1:6)

The single-minded saint, on the other hand, has the goal of the race firmly set in his heart. He knows where he is headed and has an unwavering determination to arrive there. I believe this attitude is the very thing Paul had in mind when he told the Colossians, "Were you not raised to life with Christ? Then aspire to the realm above, where Christ is, seated at the right hand of God. And let your thoughts dwell on that higher realm, not on this earthly life." (Colossians 3:1-2 NEB) The mention of this heavenly goal bears looking at in other translations:

- Aim at and seek the [*rich, eternal treasures*] that are above...(Amp)
- Reach out for the highest gifts of Heaven...(PHP)
- Set your sights on the realities of heaven...(NLT)
- Now set your sights on the rich treasures and joys of heaven...(LB)

Yes, we are headed to the land of bliss, but the condition we are in when we arrive there will mean everything to us. If a diplomat has important meetings in Moscow, he doesn't leave at the last minute and travel all night in the coach section of the plane. He would be haggard and utterly useless to accomplish his tasks. Yet it is amazing how some Christians think that just arriving to the pearly gates is all that matters!

Let us consider the inspiring words about the sanctification process written by Alexander MacLaren as we close out this chapter:

> The production in us of God-like and God-pleasing character: For this suns rise and set; for this seasons and times come and go; for this sorrows and joys are experienced; for this hopes and fears and loves are kindled. For this all the discipline of life is set in motion. For this we were created; for this we have been redeemed. For this Jesus Christ lived and suffered and died. For this God's Spirit is poured out upon the world. All else is scaffolding; this is the building which it contemplates, and when the building is reared the scaffolding may be cleared away. God means to make us like Himself.[4]

*"Seventy years are given to us! Some even live
to eighty. But even the best years are filled with pain
and trouble; soon they disappear, and we fly away...
Teach us to realize the brevity of life,
so that we may grow in wisdom."*
—Moses[1]

*"Youth is like spring, an over-praised season
more remarkable for biting winds than genial breezes.
Autumn is the mellower season, and what we
lose in flowers we more than gain in fruits."*
—Samuel Butler

THE SEASONS OF LIFE

The simple statement made by Moses provided above offers one of the most sublime thoughts which man may consider. But how many people will actually take the trouble to think about the short span of time they have on earth?

Of course, the point of this book is to encourage the reader to do this very thing: to ponder life—its brevity, its significance, its grand purposes. It is the contemplation of these weighty subjects that transports a person out of the shallow realm of the fool into the vast depths of wisdom where one discovers the solemn issues of life.

Seventy or eighty years might seem like a long time from our earthly perspective, but in light of eternity it is seen for the tiny span it actually is. In some inexplicable way, one of the key ingredients to gaining wisdom is coming into a heartfelt comprehension of that eternal perspective. "Teach us to realize the brevity of life," wrote Moses, "so that we may grow in wisdom." Some other translations bring out the meaning of this sentence more fully:

- Teach us how short our life is, so that we may become wise. (GNB)

- Teach us to number our days and recognize how few they are; help us to spend them as we should. (LB)
- So teach us to consider our mortality, so that we might live wisely. (NET)
- Teach us to count every passing day, till our hearts find wisdom. (Knox)
- Teach us then, how to interpret our existence, so that we may acquire a discerning mind. (Har)

Perhaps I could sum them all up thusly: "Lord, teach us to remove ourselves from the busyness of life long enough to really contemplate the shortness yet significance of our time on earth." Let's face it, going through life can be like being propelled down a fast-flowing river. Before you know it, you've arrived at the end and you are left wondering what happened.

Surely one of the wisest men of the early Church had to have been the apostle John. He was in his nineties when he penned his three epistles. By that time in his life, he had grasped much of what makes up a person's spiritual life. He had experienced the newfound joy of his Christian life; this eventually gave way to the long years of service to God; and finally, he had entered the wisdom of old age, where he could focus on building into the lives of others. John summed up a person's spiritual life on earth by dividing it into these three primary epochs:

> I am writing to you, little children, because your sins have been forgiven you for His name's sake. I am writing to you, fathers, because you know Him who has been from the beginning...I have written to you, young men, because you are strong, and the word of God abides in you, and you have overcome the evil one. (I John 2:12-14)

After considering "the brevity of life," John summed up man's time on earth in three basic eras: childhood, youth and fatherhood. However, before we examine these different stages of spiritual maturity, it would be good to make a couple of general observations.

First, John was describing the natural flow of a Christian's life as it *should* unfold. A person should respond to the call of God while still young. Once he has become born again, he should mature in such a way that he finds his life's calling before long and throws himself into accomplishing all he can for the kingdom of God. Having spent the better part of his adult years in this pursuit, he eventually arrives at his elder years when he has developed the necessary wisdom to guide younger believers. This is the way the Christian life typically develops when a person responds to the Lord in his youth.

However, we all know that many people don't even get saved until their latter years. And how many people have known the Lord for forty years but—spiritually speaking—are still playing in the sandbox with their toys? Just because a Christian possesses an AARP card and has been attending church for many years does not necessarily qualify him to be a spiritual father!

On the other end of the spectrum are those younger believers who are wise beyond their years. When David was but a young man, he could rightly claim, "I understand more than the aged, because I have observed Your precepts." (Psalm 119:100) And Daniel and his three companions had barely reached adulthood when it was said of them, "As for every matter of wisdom and understanding about which the king consulted them, he found them ten times better than all the magicians and conjurers who were in all his realm." (Daniel 1:20)

Although life cannot always be packaged as neatly as John laid it out, he still touched upon some very important truths about our time on earth.

SPIRITUAL CHILDHOOD

There is no question that a young person will save himself a world of trouble if he surrenders his life to Christ while still in the freshness of youth. What a terrible price many of us have paid for squandering this beautiful time of life in the cesspools of sin. "Man's mind," Oliver Wendell Holmes wrote, "once stretched by a new idea never regains its original dimension." This is certainly true of sin. There is a terrible price to pay when a young person is not content with the knowledge of good and sets himself upon a quest to learn the ways of evil. Later, if he is fortunate enough to escape the clutches of sin, he finds that he must spend the rest of his life grappling with the carnal knowledge sin had taught him. Yes, it is so much better to come to Christ while still in the bloom and innocence of youth.

And what a beautiful time of life it is when a young person discovers Jesus Christ for himself. He is in the glow of the "first love" where everything seems fresh and new! The grass is greener and the sky bluer than ever before. The Bible, which might have seemed stale and lifeless (e.g., the young person raised in church), is now energized, its words virtually jumping off the page into his heart. He senses the presence of God everywhere he turns. His worship comes alive as he sings from a rapturous heart. He sees people differently as well. Instead of seeing them through the eyes of Self—that dark perspective that reduces others to rivals who must be outdone—he sees their needs. He feels compassion and love for them.

David Ravenhill is one of my best friends and truly is a father in the faith to many people. Of this stage of the Christian life he writes:

> Just as we progress physically from children to youth, then on to adulthood, so likewise in the spiritual realm. Nobody is born fully developed physically, emotionally, or mentally. John begins by telling the Children that their sins are forgiven. Just as a baby in the natural has no past, so likewise in the spiritual realm. If a newborn could articulate why it's crying you would never hear it say "I'm

bothered by all the sins I've committed over the years." The fact is, a baby has no past to be troubled over. The newborn Christian, the moment he repents of sin and by faith takes hold of God's redeeming grace, is forgiven of his past. John then goes on to say that children know their fathers. One of the first relationships a child has is with his father. The first cry of the newborn believer is Abba or daddy/father.[2]

Yes, spiritual infancy is an exciting time of discovering the unseen realm of God. But with all of the excitement of entering into this new, spiritual life, the person is still an immature believer. Children tend to be very self-centered. The excitement they experience over this new life revolves around the blessings they are receiving from their heavenly Father. Nevertheless, God is quick to answer their prayers and flood their lives with many proofs of His love and grace.

Spiritual childhood is best characterized as a time of dependency. It is when the new believer is learning to trust God in all of the struggles and challenges of life. It is a honeymoon period when it seems that one is blessed in every area of life and all one's prayers are answered.

If the young person is progressing properly, the time will come when he will begin to broaden his horizons. Spiritual infancy has its place, but eventually his range of vision will extend beyond himself and he will become increasingly aware of other people and the enormous physical, emotional and spiritual suffering they carry through life.

SPIRITUAL YOUTH

As spiritual infancy gives way to young adulthood, the new believer finds that he must learn to exercise wisdom, fight the good fight and make his mark upon this earth. In the Garden, God imparted two great passions of life in human beings.

Women, by and large, would find their sense of fulfillment in the love of their husbands and in the joys of childbearing. Men would gain satisfaction in their life's work.

Whether or not a young person goes into fulltime ministry, the one who is properly maturing will be very conscientious of eternity's claims upon his life. He will instinctively understand that he has the opportunity and the calling to do something worthwhile with his life.

Naturally speaking, the twenty year period between the ages of 25 and 45 is the stage of life (roughly) when people are most apt to accomplish great things. John says that people in this season of life "are strong." It is then that the person comes into his own. It is not only a time of youthful strength but also a time of courage. No mountain is too high to conquer; no foe is too powerful to vanquish. Indeed, John says that they have "overcome the evil one."

Not only have they victoriously stood toe-to-toe with the enemy regarding their own particular struggles, but they have learned how to fight for the sake of others.

This is the time in life when a young man can undertake a new Christian work, go off to a distant land to share the gospel, evangelize a country or minister to a group of people in need. It is a time when ministers build effective ministries; pastors reach their zenith in shepherding a flock. The great works of God have been built upon the back of this younger generation.

Paul Washer recently shared an impassioned message about eternal values with a group of youth pastors. In it he said this:

> This life is a vapor. I am 47-years-old, but yesterday I was 21; where did it all go? I praise God that as a young man I spent myself in the Andes Mountains and the jungles of Peru doing what I no longer have the strength to do. While you're still a young man, while you still have strength in you, labor with all your might!

SPIRITUAL MATURITY

Where would the Church be without the vigor and tenacity of those younger generations? And yet, I would say that the spiritual father plays just as significant a role in the furtherance of the kingdom of God. Their part may be played out quietly behind the scenes, but it is nonetheless vital in the grand scheme of things. Rightly did Solomon say, "The glory of young men is their strength, and the honor of old men is their gray hair." (Proverbs 20:29)

For all of the great accomplishments that occur in the younger years, all too often they are unfortunately accompanied by many mistakes and failures. What the aged man lacks in energy and physical vigor, he makes up for in wisdom. True, a younger man may accomplish five projects for every one an elderly man sees completed; but just as true is that the younger man typically wastes a lot of time and energy. I cringe thinking about how many times in my younger days I rushed headstrong down some path only to discover that it wasn't God's will. The Lord is exceedingly patient with the sincere young man who makes mistakes, but the spiritual father has learned through these painful experiences to be more prudent. As Solomon said: "The wise are cautious and avoid danger; fools plunge ahead with reckless confidence." (Proverbs 14:16 NLT)

Another area of maturation is that of understanding the issues of life. Someone once said, "Early in life as a student I thought I knew everything; later, nothing; still later, something." It is clear to me that the man who wrote those words had been properly humbled by the mistakes of his younger days. His concise statement sums up the entirety of the process one undergoes in transferring his trust from himself to the Lord.

It is so true that youth typically have an exaggerated perspective of the extent of their wisdom. As someone else quipped, "If you want to know something, ask a teenager while they still know everything." This line of thinking is true in a spiritual sense as well. Immature believers also tend to see themselves far beyond their actual level of spiritual maturity. What's worse is that when they are in this early stage, they often are so prideful that they will not accept the kind of correction that could actually help them to grow.

Nevertheless, the sincere believer learns from his mistakes. He has been humbled by poor decisions and faulty opinions time and again. If he is properly progressing, he will develop a mindset of great distrust in his own thinking. He becomes much more cautious about throwing around the pat answers he freely dispensed earlier in life.

This phase of self-doubt is crucial to the maturing process because it fosters true dependency upon God. Over time, the believer emerges from this period with a newfound confidence—not in himself but in his ability to follow the leading of the Holy Spirit. Not only this, but he has also learned to be more reticent about offering advice to others. When he does share something, it tends to be wise and meaningful.

Another benefit of this aging process is the growing ability to discern what is truly important in life. I think C. H. Spurgeon was correct when he said, "A babe in grace knows twenty things: a young man in Christ knows ten things: but a father in Christ knows one thing, and that one thing he knows thoroughly. Oh, to have one heart, one eye, for our one Lord, and for Him alone!"[3]

The ambition to succeed and accomplish (with all their mixed motives) begins to diminish. Worldly positions start to lose their luster as a person comes into the latter stages of life. The old veteran, who has fought through some of the great battles of life, knows all too well the vanity of the world's offerings, the misery of sin and the deep fulfillment of walking with God.

An interesting aspect of this transformation is that many ministers who have the gift of teaching undergo a metamorphosis from being someone who *instructs* to one who *imparts* spiritual knowledge. If the man has been on the path to maturity, chances are he has taught many good things over his years in ministry. But as he crosses into spiritual fatherhood, his teachings tend to bypass the intellect and find lodging in the listener's heart.

Perhaps the most significant change the aging believer undergoes is the sweet softening of his spirit. One old-time minister sums up this transformation:

> Little by little with time the eyes get open. Our lips are not as ready with criticism and judgment as of yore. With no less zeal for God and His cause, yet it is now a zeal according to knowledge. The moderation is not a cooling off of religious experience, nor a curtailing of work, nor a withholding of testimony. It is, instead, a deliverance from hastiness of judgment, jumping to conclusions, and quickness to speak severely of others. It is the departure of a domineering, autocratic spirit and manner. It is the correcting of pure love, the mellowing of the Christian into a calm-eyed, level-headed, sweet-hearted, kindly-tongued man.[4]

Another writer adds: "Self-control has ripened into self-conquest; kindness has been hallowed into love; the heavy morning of self-denial has brightened into the cloudless day of self-repose; the toil of the ascent has been repaid by the landscape from the summit."[5]

Yes, old age for the Christian is a blessed period of life. What a joy it is for the old veteran to look back over his life with the satisfaction that he has done his utmost to promote the cause of Christ. Whether or not he was recognized by others for his life of service, he knows that he is hastening toward the day when he will hear, "Well done, thou faithful servant." He can now look forward to the world to come.

> *"When as a child, I laughed and wept, Time crept.*
> *When as a youth, I dreamed and talked, Time walked.*
> *When I became a full-grown man, Time ran.*
> *And later, as I older grew, Time flew.*
> *Soon I shall find while traveling on, Time gone."[6]*

"*Dost thou love life? Then do not squander time, for that's the stuff life is made of.*"
—*Benjamin Franklin*[1]

"*Live life, then, with a due sense of responsibility, not as men who do not know the meaning and purpose of life but as those who do. Make the best use of your time, despite all the difficulties of these days. Don't be vague but firmly grasp what you know to be the will of God.*"
—*The Apostle Paul*[2]

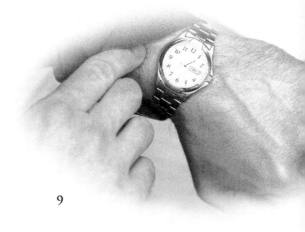

REDEEMING THE TIME

I suppose at some level we must all decide where our loyalties lie. If we are primarily living for what this world offers, then let us throw off all unnecessary restraint and live for whatever pleasure we can derive from each moment. However, if we are destined for another realm, then we must incorporate into our lives the value system of that realm.

Earth life thinks in temporal terms. The message constantly conveyed by the world's pitchmen is that we owe it to ourselves to gain all of the pleasure we can possibly extract from life. Other people are only as important as they play a role in helping us achieve that temporary happiness.* Possessions are rated very high in earth's economy because they play a role in our sense of security and happiness. Human success is lauded as something of great import: those considered "great" being the ones who achieve the most fame, pleasure and power in this world.

Heaven has an economy that is vastly different and superior to what this world promotes. In fact, the Bible tells

---

* How tragic that some ministers see people in this light.

us that the passion for pleasure, possessions and position is, in itself, wrong. Take a few moments of your time to chew on the significance of Heaven's perspective of earth life as it is presented in First John 2:15-17. I offer it in two translations you may not be familiar with to help you see it in a fresh light.

> Never give your hearts to this world or to any of the things in it. A man cannot love the Father and love the world at the same time. For the whole world-system, based as it is on men's primitive desires, their greedy ambitions and the glamour of all that they think splendid, is not derived from the Father at all, but from the world itself. The world and all its passionate desires will one day disappear. But the man who is following God's will is part of the permanent and cannot die. (PHP)

> Do not set your hearts on the godless world or anything in it. Anyone who loves the world is a stranger to the Father's love. Everything the world affords, all that panders to the appetites or entices the eyes, all the glamour of its life, springs not from the Father but from the godless world. And that world is passing away with all its allurements, but he who does God's will stands forevermore. (NEB)

What stands out in John's statements—regardless of the version you prefer—is that the Lord's perspective on the things of earth is much different than man's. Let's face it: all the devil has to offer mankind are those worldly charms that gratify the lower nature. But his entire system is built upon a massive deception. People struggle through life, always grasping after an elusive sense of satisfaction the world cannot provide. They have been blinded by the enemy to the meaningful and fulfilling life to which God has called them.

"Redeem the time" is terminology borrowed from the King James Version of Ephesians 5:16, of course. The very word "redeem" instantly ushers our thinking back to the frightful condition earth life had dealt us. There we were, slaving away in Satan's prison camp—kept going each day by some morsel of temporary and unsatisfying pleasure—until the Redeemer purchased our souls and rescued us from that wretched life of servitude.†

Satan's great lie is that living for self satisfies, when actually it only makes one increasingly more miserable. By contrast, God offers His followers an unselfish life of helping other people— the very kind of lifestyle that brings one true fulfillment. One of the great questions that our probationary period on earth is meant to answer is: Did we squander the time we were allotted living for the allurements of this world or did we utilize our time valuing and helping others?

Paul tells us to "redeem the time." I believe that the apostle purposely used this terminology to illustrate an important aspect of the way we live our lives. Perhaps I can offer an expanded version of what I believe he was saying: "For many years you frittered your time away living for yourself. Of course, you cannot redeem that time, as once time is lost, it is lost forever. However, you can 'make up for lost time' by using your remaining years doing good to others and bringing joy to your Redeemer."

FINANCIAL COMPARISONS

The truth is that time is a spendable commodity. It could be said that we have been given a disbursement account (e.g., Parable

---

† I realize that many people are raised in Christian homes and don't recall their lives being spent this way. Nevertheless, until the Savior actually purchased their souls, they were very much a part of the world system. Self-love, self-righteousness and all of the other forms of sin that lurk in the human heart are just as much a part of Satan's realm as are the more blatant types of sin such as immorality and drunkenness.

of the Talents) to determine how we will employ it. Indeed, it is amazing how many similarities money and time share.

For instance, both are divided into measurable units. Our viewpoint of money is determined by the situation at hand. If we are purchasing a pack of gum, we think in terms of pennies. If we are going out to dinner, thirty or forty dollars will typically suffice. If we need a new refrigerator, we may spend as much as a thousand dollars. If we are considering the purchase of a new home, our life's savings may be required.

Time has its own measuring system. We may only be able to spare a few minutes during the day to call a loved one. An hour watching one's son play baseball is considered "time well spent" for the boy's emotional wellbeing. A cross-country trip may only take two weeks of vacation time, while a stint in the army would entail two years. A career position may necessitate thirty or more years of our lives.

"Redeem the time," is the language of economics. To purchase something means that the seller will exchange the item for a certain amount of money. Likewise, to gain moments, hours or longer portions of time for the sake of Christ means that time spent on something else must be surrendered.

Time plays such an essential role in the kingdom of heaven that one could almost use the terms interchangeably: Time is like "a treasure hidden in the field, which a man found and hid again; and from joy over it he goes and sells all that he has and buys that field." Again, it is like "a merchant seeking fine pearls, and upon finding one pearl of great value, he went and sold all that he had and bought it." (Matthew 13:44-46)

A person who values time spends it wisely. One minister wrote, "The apostle bids us 'buy up' out of the market what we can never purchase so cheaply again—what, in fact, we can never buy again at any price."[3] One example of this truth that comes to mind is a contractor renting a backhoe for four hours at the cost of several hundred dollars. He will be sure to get his money's worth out of it. When a person is "on the clock" for something that expensive, he doesn't stand around with his workers kidding and cutting up.

Yet, there is always the temptation to see both time and money as being unlimited. When we gaze off into the future, it seems as though days without end lay before us. We tend to allow circumstances to carry us along, precious moments coming and going as if they were mere pennies. The reality is that we only have so much time; one day our opportunities on earth will be over. "We are always complaining that our days are few," said the Roman philosopher Seneca, "and acting as though there would be no end of them."

It is this sense of time being endless that allows many to squander it. We are all afforded the same number of minutes per day and days per week. How we "spend" those precious moments will determine the course of our lives. As Maria Edgeworth quipped, "If we take care of the moments, the years will take care of themselves."

Those who have been most successful in the work of saving souls have been singular for their wise use of time. Whatever their particular ministry, and wherever it was accomplished, the one thing they all held in common is that they spent every possible moment advancing the cause in which they were involved. Weeks are planned out with precision. Some are so disciplined that even leisure time and vacations are scheduled. Such people can typically look back over the course of their lives with the satisfaction that they made the most of their opportunity on earth. As Henry Longfellow penned:

> *Lives of great men all remind us,*
> *We can make our lives sublime,*
> *And, departing, leave behind us*
> *Footprints on the sands of time.*[4]

Aren't the lives of God's champions a fulfillment of Paul's injunction? "Live life, then, with a due sense of responsibility, not as men who do not know the meaning and purpose of life but as those who do. Make the best use of your time, despite all the difficulties of these days." (Ephesians 5:15-16 PHP)

"Time is so short," said Jonathan Edwards, "and the work which we have to do in it is so great, that we have none of it to spare."[5]

By contrast are those who fritter their time away like a frivolous rich kid who can't spend his father's money fast enough. They act as though the supply is endless. However, squandered hours accumulate into wasted years. Before they know it life has passed them by. They have missed their chance and have nothing but regret to carry with them into eternity.

"Time wasted is a theft from God," someone else once said.[6] "Know the true value of time;" said Lord Chesterfield, "snatch, seize, and enjoy every moment of it. No idleness, no laziness, no procrastination. Never put off till tomorrow what you can do today."[7] One old time minister wrote:

> Time is life's freightage, wherewith some men trade and make a fortune; and others waste in extravagance. Time is life's book, out of which some extract wondrous wisdom; while others let it lie uncovered, and then die fools. Time is life's tree, from which some gather precious fruit, while others lie down under its shadow, and perish with hunger. Time is life's ladder, whereby some raise themselves up to honor, and renown, and glory; and some let themselves down into the deeps of shame, degradation, and ignominy. Time will be to us what, by our use of the treasure, we make it; a good or an evil, a blessing or a curse.[8]

There is one final comparison between money and time that must be considered. Neither of them have any value in themselves other than as a means to a higher end. The purpose for the period of existence we have been allotted on this planet can be summed up in a handful of great purposes. Perhaps I could encapsulate the point of it all in some simple biblical mandates:

- Spend time expressing your love and adoration of God.
- Spend time doing deeds of mercy to those in need.
- Spend time in God's Word.
- Spend time interceding for others.
- Spend time in such a way that God is glorified by it.
- Spend time showing love to those around you.
- Spend time waiting on God.
- Spend time allowing the Holy Spirit to mold you into the image of Christ.
- Spend time preparing for life in the hereafter.

When God laid out the economic plan He expected His children to live by, He asked them to give back to Him and His work one dollar out of every ten that were earned. Indeed, the word tithe is a derivative of the word tenth.

His demand upon our time was even greater, asking for one seventh rather than one tenth. This principle was so important in His economy that He included it in the Ten Commandments. In the same way that God tends to bless our financial generosity, so too does He with our time.

The Jewish exiles who returned to Jerusalem from Babylon learned this lesson the hard way. They couldn't understand why everything kept going wrong. Nothing ever seemed to work out the way they had hoped. After allowing this frustration to mount within them over a few months, the Lord spoke to them through the prophet Haggai. He said, "You have sown much, but harvest little; you eat, but there is not enough to be satisfied; you drink, but there is not enough to become drunk; you put on clothing, but no one is warm enough; and he who earns, earns wages to put into a purse with holes...You look for much, but behold, it comes to little." (Haggai 1:6-9) He then went on to tell them that the reason their lives felt cursed was because they had neglected His injunction to rebuild the Temple. Instead, they had spent their time pursuing their personal ambitions.

This is a good reminder to those of us who seem to constantly face hardship. Perhaps you aren't giving God the first fruits of your money and time. On the other hand, those who have spent their time and money well will finish their lives with great satisfaction.

Someone once suggested that Christians should evaluate their activities through the lens of two essential questions: Will what I'm doing matter five years from now? Will it bear any significance on eternity?

Many of the things we do would not pass that test, and if we took it seriously, I suspect we'd find that we have a lot more time to spend on things that really matter. As John said, "The world and all its passionate desires will one day disappear. But the man who is following God's will is part of the permanent and cannot die." (I John 2:17 PHP)

REVISITING THE TERM KAIROS

Paul tells his readers to redeem, or purchase, or barter for, not *chronos*—a period of time—but *kairos*, the opportune time, the time that is for a particular season. Expending our efforts toward godly things in general certainly has its place. As we will discuss in the following chapter, it is right to purposely set aside periods of time for the furtherance of one's spiritual life.

The aged apostle certainly would not have been amiss to tell us to redeem our *chronos*. He could have taught the importance of making certain that periods of our lives—whether measured in hours or years—be spent in the furtherance of spiritual priorities.

Instead, his emphasis had more to do with certain

opportunities we would encounter in life. In Chapter Five, I mentioned "the law of opportunity." This states that we must be careful to capitalize on the opportunities the Lord sends our way.

For instance, I know Christians who never mature spiritually because they simply will not acknowledge their sins and repent of them. Year after year drifts by and they remain unchanged. While others around them are growing and advancing in the spiritual life, they remain stuck at the starting gate because they do not have the courage to face their faults and deal with them. What is so sad is that the Lord has graciously provided them with many different occasions to repent, but they carelessly squandered each one. They just did not value those different *kairos* moments God afforded them.

Another type of opportunity that comes along in life is in the realm of Christian service. Perhaps you have been in some situation with an unbeliever when suddenly you felt compelled to share your testimony with him. While you never found out if anything came of that conversation, you still walked away from it with the sense that you had done the right thing. You experienced exactly what Paul was referring to when he wrote, "Conduct yourselves with wisdom toward outsiders, making the most of the opportunity (*kairos*). Let your speech always be with grace, as though seasoned with salt, so that you will know how you should respond to each person." (Colossians 4:5-6) Some opportunities will only present themselves once in a lifetime— and so much might be at stake for the other person!

Just as important are those situations that occasionally come up when we are able to speak a timely word to another Christian. One brother might need you to lovingly confront him about obvious sin in his life. If this is done in love, it can powerfully alter a person's life. Someone else may need that word of encouragement that you are in a unique position to bring. Either way, the proverb holds true: "Like apples of gold in settings of silver is a word spoken in right circumstances." (Proverbs 25:11)

Then there are those special times when the spiritual (atmospheric) conditions are just right to really enter into the presence of God. If you are blessed with a worship leader and a congregation who truly thirst for the Lord's presence, there will be certain worship times when heaven seems to come down to earth. If you are led by the Spirit, you will quickly enter into that wonderful atmosphere and allow it to cleanse your soul and refresh your spirit. If you tend to go through life in the flesh, you may sense that something special is occurring around you, but you will not have the capacity to benefit from it for yourself.

There are also those special occurrences when the pages of the Bible seem to be electrified with life. This typically occurs when there is a body of believers present who are sincerely seeking God's presence. When the Lord draws near in those special times, His Word seems to jump off the page at the reader.

These are only a few examples of how the Lord may provide you with a special *kairos* along the journey of life. They are golden opportunities to deepen your life with Him and to have a positive and enduring effect on the lives of other people. And, of course, it should be noted that we will be held accountable for the way we handled those situations.

It is true, we have all squandered so much time. It is precious, uncertain and in short supply. Yet, we still have today in which to make up for time poorly spent. Let us make the most of every opportunity; let us redeem the time.

"Lord, I have called daily upon You;
I have stretched out my hands to You."
—The Psalmist[1]

"What I do today is important
because I'm exchanging a day of my life for it."
—Anonymous [2]

FRUIT FROM THE DAILY LIFE

L ife, as we learned earlier, is one long string of 24-hour periods—i.e., an accumulation of dots on our timeline. One day tends to blend into another, establishing a pattern of life and eventually a destiny. Thus, the way we spend our days is of vital importance. A sincere believer is always willing to take an honest evaluation of his life. A good place to begin is with a simple question: What kind of fruit is my daily life producing?

Most Christians don't tend to consider this question until the subject is raised through a sermon or a book. Perhaps the person's pastor preaches on the need to share one's faith with unbelievers. In the midst of the message, the preacher makes the point about how Christians should have fruit to show for their lives.

The Christian feels convicted by the message and immediately begins to put forth a real effort at witnessing. He buys some tracts, starts knocking on doors, sharing with people the Four Gospel Laws. While he is engaged in such activities the concerns he has felt over the lack of fruit coming from his life are alleviated. Usually such efforts prove to be short lived, however. As the conviction of the sermon wanes, so do the person's activities. As his works decrease, the old, nagging feelings of not doing enough to satisfy God begin to reemerge.

Or maybe he reads a book about the need to love other people. The author rightly points out that love is the most prominent fruit of the Spirit mentioned in Galatians 5. Once again the man senses something amiss in his spiritual life and attempts to correct himself by showing more kindness to his family and co-workers. He might even do something radical like get involved with a local soup kitchen. However, it isn't long before the message of the book is crowded out of his thinking by the many occupations of his busy life and he falls back into his old rut. Before he knows it, he's back to being impatient with his kids and unconcerned about the lost souls down on Skid Row.

The problem here is that the man is attempting to correct something that he does not have the capacity to correct. If a Christian wants to have luscious looking fruit hanging off his tree, he must submit himself to the process that produces it.

FRUIT BEARING

Every healthy Christian bears fruit. Jesus said as much when He said, "I am the vine, you are the branches; he who abides in Me, and I in him, he bears much fruit..." (John 15:5) In the parable about the different soil types, Jesus said that the man who received the gospel with a good heart brings forth "a good crop, a hundred, sixty or thirty times what was sown." (Matthew 13:23 PHP) Both metaphors make the point that the natural progression of the Christian life is to "bear much fruit."

There are two important inferences in the illustration of the Vine. The first one is that the branch is an offshoot of the Vine. It isn't some foreign element that has been grafted in.* It is as

---

* Paul used the metaphor of grafting a foreign branch onto a tree to show the preeminent position the Jewish nation has as God's people. Gentiles have been grafted into the family of God because of Jewish unbelief. In other words, he was using the metaphor to make a different point.

much a part of the Vine as one's arm is part of one's body.

The same point is made with the seed. God created both animal and vegetable life to reproduce itself through the process of yielding seed. "The earth brought forth vegetation, plants yielding seed after their kind, and trees bearing fruit with seed in them, after their kind...God made the beasts of the earth after their kind, and the cattle after their kind, and everything that creeps on the ground after its kind..." (Genesis 1:12, 25) In other words, every form of life reproduces itself; it does not have the capacity to produce something other than what it is.

Peter wrote, "for you have been born again not of seed which is perishable but imperishable, that is, through the living and enduring word of God." (I Peter 1:23) That word is actually the Spirit of Christ, implanted into a person's heart. In the same way that a seed planted in a field will produce a plant after its own kind, so too will the indwelling Holy Spirit bring forth the life of God within a believer. This is what Peter meant when he later said that the believer has become a partaker "of the divine nature." (II Peter 1:5)

One can see this regarding one's moral behavior. For instance, the apostle John wrote, "The person who has been born into God's family does not make a practice of sinning because now God's life is in him; so he can't keep on sinning, for this new life has been born into him and controls him—he has been *born again.*" (I John 3:9 LB; italics in the original) Jesus made the same point when discussing true and false teachers. He said, "A good tree cannot produce bad fruit, nor can a bad tree produce good fruit...you will know them by their fruits." (Matthew 7:18, 20)

The point is that if the seed of God has been implanted in a human heart, it cannot help but produce the life of God. It isn't something that must be forced or conjured up. It is simply *there* and the actions coming forth from it will correspond with its inherent nature. The believer only needs to tap into that Source that is within him.

When He addressed the issue of false teachers, Jesus began by saying, "Beware of the false prophets, who come to you in sheep's clothing, but inwardly are ravenous wolves." (Matthew 7:15) Someone who is false may be able to imitate the behavior of a sheep, but he does not have the sheep's nature. He is a wolf attempting to pass himself off as a sheep. It is not any more difficult for a sheep to be mild mannered than it is for a wolf to be cruel. Both are simply being true to their natures.

Of course, the person who has experienced rebirth still must resist the ways of the old nature. But it isn't completely forced. If the seed of Jesus Christ has been implanted in his heart, he will feel compelled to go against the fallen nature.

The second inference in the metaphor of the Vine is as important as the first. The branch attached to the Vine must be nourished by the sap that comes from the Vine. If the branch does not stay connected—if it is snapped off, for instance—it cannot continue to receive the needed sustenance that comes from the Vine.

However, if it is attached, vitality will simply flow into it, and fruit will be the natural outcome. "I am the vine, you are the branches; he who abides in Me, and I in him, he bears much fruit..." If there is no fruit hanging off the branches, something is clearly wrong. To discover the cause, we must "go to the root of the problem."

THE ROOT SYSTEM

Every tree has a root system. Just as a building is only as strong as its foundation, so too a tree will only be as healthy as its root system. Solomon assures us that "the root of the righteous yields fruit." (Proverbs 12:12) Paul said, "...if the root is holy, the branches are too." (Romans 11:16) Isaiah spoke of those who would "take root downward and bear fruit upward." (Isaiah 37:31) In the Parable of the Sower and the Seed, Jesus said that those who possess only a "temporary" faith are like a plant that "withered away...because they had no root." (Matthew 13:6, 21)

If the tree represents our spiritual life and the fruit

represents what comes out of that life, what role does the root play in the process? The main function of the root system is to absorb nutrients that are, in turn, channeled into the tree. This is a vital part of the life process for the believer as well. In our case, the five senses act as our roots and the heart is the storage unit that receives and dispenses spiritual nutrition.[†]

Roots do not forage for food like an animal would; they simply absorb whatever the soil contains. As Jesus said, "Observe how the lilies of the field grow; they do not toil nor do they spin…" (Matthew 6:38) The roots lay in the soil and soak up what comes to them through the moisture.

The Psalmist used this metaphor to contrast the person who spends time in the Word of God with the one who subjects himself to the influences of ungodly people.

> Blessed…is the man who walks and lives not in the counsel of the ungodly (following their advice, their plans and purposes), nor stands (submissive and inactive) in the path where sinners walk, nor sits down (to relax and rest) where the scornful (and the mockers) gather. But his delight and desire are in the law of the Lord, and on His law (the precepts, the instructions, the teachings of God) he habitually meditates (ponders and studies) by day and by night. And he shall be like a tree firmly planted (and tended) by the streams of water, ready to bring forth its fruit in its season; its leaf also shall not fade or wither; and everything he does shall prosper (and come to maturity). (Psalm 1:1-2 Amp)

The contrast stands out starkly. The passive person hangs around ungodly people "submissive and inactive" while the godly man diligently spends time in Scripture. The Psalmist is clearly bringing out how susceptible the human heart is to outside influ-

---

† This dynamic also holds true regarding negative spiritual influences—as we shall soon see.

ences. Solomon would later warn, "Guard your heart above all else, for it determines the course of your life." (Proverbs 4:23 NLT)

There is a constant war raging within man's thinking. The Prince of the Power of the Air relentlessly attempts to draw people into atmospheres he has created for the express purpose of coloring people's minds with his dark wisdom. Satan has created miasmas of evil all over planet Earth.

A Christian may not indulge himself in "the deep things of Satan" (Revelation 2:24), but if he is subjecting himself to the enemy's polluted atmospheres through television, the Internet, and so on, he will still become increasingly contaminated.

Allow me to illustrate this truth with a refrigerator. The food a person puts in it will tend to take on the odors of whatever pungent items might be present. To the degree they are contaminated by these smells depends on two things: how smelly the offending item is and how long the food is exposed to it.

If I split open a white onion and leave it on the middle shelf of the refrigerator for five minutes, the effects on the other food would be minimal. However, if I leave it in there overnight, that smell will begin to permeate the other food. By comparison, if I put a piece of rotten fish in the same spot, it won't take long at all before the other food takes on its rancid smell.

And so it is when we spend time in the foul atmosphere of the devil. In the spiritual realm he carries with him a stench not unlike that of rotted flesh. It wouldn't surprise me if angels had the ability to smell demons in their vicinity.‡

To bury one's roots into soil that has been saturated with the world's food, is like a small tree planted in soil that has been saturated with weed killer. True, that poison won't kill something as large as a tree immediately, but it will certainly stunt its growth and set into motion a long, slow death.

God has created our hearts to be highly impressionable, and time plays a key role in that process. If we spend lengthy

---

‡ The reverse of this spiritual truth can be seen in the "fragrance" of godly behavior: II Corinthians 2:15; Ephesians 5:2; Philippians 4:18.

periods of time focusing our minds upon the truth found in the Word of God, our hearts will gradually be molded into the God-mentality offered in Scripture. Likewise, if we spend time soaking in the atmosphere of the world, we can expect our inner life to take on its rank odor.

THE IMPORTANT ROLE OF CHRONOS

In the last chapter we saw the value of taking advantage of those *kairos* moments that occasionally present themselves in life. Now we can see the important part *chronos* plays in our Christian lives. *Kairos* has its place in the life of the maturing Christian, but there are some aspects of spiritual growth that *only* come through *chronos*.

One cannot force *kairos* situations; for the most part they are not within our control. We simply must respond to them as they present themselves.

However, we tend to have a greater degree of control over *chronos.* One could even say that one's lifetime is simply one long *chronos*—to be divided up and used however one sees fit. Simple decisions like how one uses his time plays an extremely important part in the Christian life.

Someone once said, "Time is the substance of life. When anyone asks you to give your time, they're really asking for a chunk of your life."[3] That is very true; and what I would add to it is that the Lord is making that request of His people. He expects us to take time to interact with Him; to spend time with Him; to give periods of our lives to Him.

Oswald Chambers didn't have much patience when Christians complained about not having the time to spend with the Lord. "'I haven't time!' Of course you have time!" he exclaimed. "Take time, strangle some other interests and make time to realize that the center of power in your life is the Lord Jesus Christ and His Atonement."[4]

The fact of the matter is that there are no shortcuts when it comes to growing fruit. It only comes about through spending time with God—in His Word and in His presence.

Let's face it: spending time in prayer, worship and the Word of God is not desirable to the flesh. It requires discipline to establish such a habit.

For years, through preaching and writing, I have championed the cause of maintaining a vibrant devotional life. One of the practical aspects to establishing this practice is to faithfully spend a set amount of time each day with the Lord. One of the criticisms I have received about this practice is that spending time in study or prayer does not guarantee that it will be quality time. It is interesting to me that the people who make this argument seem to have had little or no experience in actually doing it. And they rarely offer a worthwhile alternative.

It is true that putting oneself in a place of prayer doesn't necessarily mean that the person will actually connect with God. The alternative is for him to pray when he feels like praying. Considering the carnal nature's lack of interest in the things of God, it would be spiritual suicide to build a prayer life around the fluctuations of our feelings.§

There is no question that the most effective use of our time on earth is prayer. Christians simply must set aside *chronos* periods to be connected to the Vine. As A.W. Tozer so pointedly puts it, "The Christian who is satisfied to give God His 'minute' and to have 'a little talk with Jesus' is the same one who shows up at the evangelistic service weeping over his retarded spiritual growth and begging the evangelist to show him the way out of his difficulty."[5]

S.D. Gordon wrote, "The great people of the earth today are the people...who take time and pray. They have not time. It must be taken from something else. This something else is important. Very important, and pressing, but still less important and less

---

§ It also robs the person of one of the great gifts God has bestowed upon mankind: habit. Practice anything long enough and before long it becomes a habit. Building a vibrant devotional life only comes about by remaining faithful to it—every day.

pressing than prayer…We need time for prayer, unhurried time, daily time, time enough to forget about how much time it is."[6]

His comment reminds us of one of the points of the last chapter: "…to gain moments, hours or longer portions of time for the sake of Christ means that time spent on something else must be surrendered."

Another minister encouraged prayer by making a different point: "Let us never forget that the greatest thing we can do for God or for man is to pray. For we can accomplish far more by our prayers than by our work. Prayer is omnipotent; it can do anything that God can do! When we pray God works. All fruitfulness in service is the outcome of prayer…"[7]

In referring to the great saints of Church history, E.M. Bounds wrote: "They prayed much, prayed long, and drank deeper and deeper still. They asked, they sought, and they knocked, till heaven opened its richest inner treasures of grace to them…They took time to be alone with God. Their praying was no hurried performance."[8]

And finally, Leonard Ravenhill cried, "Where, oh where are the tears over this lust-bound age of sinners, over the lost millions in heathen lands, and over the cultured pagans on our own doorsteps? We would like to weep, but we are too busy and at the moment have too much of the dust of Time in our eyes to get the tears of Eternity moving."[9]

I offer these statements to rouse the reader to prayer; but I also have included them here to show that this is what godly leaders have always lived and taught. Whatever our level of commitment might be, let us at least acknowledge that the sentiments expressed by these men are what we should all aspire to and actively work toward.

One day—and that Day is as certain as death—we will all present our timelines for examination by the Lord. That string of days—with all of its *kairos* moments and *chronos* periods—represents our time on earth. Oh, let us do our utmost to set aside those periods in which we can soak in the vital truths of Scripture and spend time in the beautiful aroma of His presence. So much depends on it.

"In my opinion whatever we may have to go through now is less than nothing compared with the magnificent future God has planned for us."
–The Apostle Paul[1]

"I'm not afraid of storms, for I am learning how to sail my ship."
–Aeschylus

WEATHERING THE STORMS

hen we have reached the final day of our timeline and we slip into the hereafter, there will be one thing God will be looking for: evidence that shows we possess a genuine faith in Jesus Christ. Not only will that faith gain us entrance into God's eternal dwelling place, but it is also the one gift we can present to the One who purchased our salvation.

Faith is not primarily one's assent to the orthodox teachings of Christianity. It is the heart-felt trust one person has in another. It is intensely personal and is borne out of a deep relationship that grows over the course of time as two people prove their loyalty to each other. That kind of trust is built by going through difficult experiences together and learning how the other person handles himself in life.

When I stepped down from the position of president of Pure Life Ministries, without hesitation I immediately named Jeff Colón my successor. I knew from having gone through many storms with him that he was a faithful Christian and a trustworthy leader.

Our faith in Christ is deepened and proven in much the same

way. Any true believer discovers God's faithfulness over time. This doesn't come primarily through hearing stories about His trustworthiness but by experiencing it for oneself. Over time, a deep sense of trust for the Lord builds in a believer's heart— even to the point that he can handle difficult circumstances without becoming unsettled in his trust in God.

To understand the point of all of this, we must consider it from God's perspective. Down through the history of mankind, no one has been as misrepresented, falsely accused and slandered as the Lord. This dark cynicism about His character has reached its zenith in our generation. I have a picture in my mind of Jesus standing in a vast auditorium in front of a multitude of un-believers, who are hurling all kinds of slanderous accusations at Him. One can only imagine what it would mean to Him to have one of His followers stand up in the midst of that hostile mob and exclaim with everything in him, "Lord, I don't care what they say about You; I believe in You!"

Of course, it takes time to establish that kind of belief in God's character. One would naturally expect that this type of faith comes about as the Lord lavishes the follower with countless assurances of His trustworthiness. And God does this for the baby Christian. But when the Lord begins to deepen a person's faith, He does it in a surprising way: He purposely puts the person into situations that make it difficult to believe in Him! In other words, He stretches a person's faith.

One picture of this dynamic is that of a weightlifter. He doesn't grow stronger by taking it easy on his muscles. No, precisely the opposite! He grows stronger by abusing his body through strenuous exercise. If he wants his arms to grow more muscular, he does certain exercises that exhaust his biceps, triceps and forearms. By the time he has concluded his weightlifting session his arms are so fatigued that he can hardly pick up a ten pound box.

This perfectly illustrates the difference in perspective from a "Live-for-Now" person and an eternally-minded believer. The nearsighted guy wants to take it easy on himself so he can effortlessly pick up the ten-pound boxes of life. The very ease of picking up that small package reinforces the notion that he is strong. By contrast, the guy who goes through life with a long-term perspective has regular sessions in the gym so he can strengthen his muscles and be prepared to handle fifty-pound boxes when necessary.

So, too, God puts us in situations where our faith seems to be pushed to its very limit of endurance. But it is through that very kind of stress that a person's faith grows stronger and deeper. Surely this is what James was referring to when he wrote: "When all kinds of trials and temptations crowd into your lives my brothers, don't resent them as intruders, but welcome them as friends! Realize that they come to test your faith and to produce in you the quality of endurance. But let the process go on until that endurance is fully developed, and you will find you have become men of mature character..." (James 1:2-4 PHP)

Another aspect to this faith-building program is that our wise heavenly Father knows how to build our faith over time. Another way to illustrate how all this works can be seen in the realm of boxing. Consider the case of a trainer who runs a boxing gym downtown. One day a teenager comes in asking to be trained. The old coach puts the kid in front of a heavy bag and has him throw some punches. What stands out immediately is that the young man is unusually talented. He is certainly raw and untaught, but he possesses remarkable speed and power in his punches.

In spite of the kid's natural ability, the trainer doesn't sign him up for the fight card taking place at the local auditorium Saturday night. No, he spends months teaching him how to hold his fists, how to ward off punches, how to hit the bag with all his might and so on. He eventually signs him up to participate in amateur bouts. After engaging in at least twenty of these contests, the young man is finally allowed to participate in his first professional match. As he begins winning fights, the trainer gradually increases the quality of the boxers he will face. Eventually the kid begins participating in main events. And then finally, after years of training and fighting, he is given the opportunity to fight the world champion.

By this point, he knows what its like to get hit in the stomach so hard the wind goes out of him; to weather a flurry of punches to the head; to get back up after being knocked down. He has become a seasoned fighter. That kind of skill doesn't come by watching training videos but through a great deal of painful experience.

Here again we find the element of time. There is a reason a boxing match lasts for 12-15 rounds: it allows enough time for the better fighter to prove himself over the course of the bout. There have always been "one round marvels" who can dazzle the audience for three minutes; but a boxer has to be able to endure all the way to the end of a grueling fight to win the championship.

All of this is a picture of how our heavenly Father trains His children and deepens their faith. God doesn't throw a spiritual infant into the ring with the champion. He allows his faith to grow by facing increasingly more violent storms in life. Each new experience strengthens his faith. The more difficult the level of training, the deeper the person will go in his relationship with God. Charles Spurgeon said it this way:

> Faith is a sound sea-going vessel, and was not meant to lie in dock and perish of dry rot...And if God give thee great faith, my dear brother, thou must expect great trials; for, in proportion as thy faith shall grow, thou wilt have to do more, and endure more. Little boats may keep close to shore, as become little boats; but if God make thee a great vessel, and load

thee with a rich freight, He means that thou shouldest know what great billows are and should feel their fury till thou seest His wonders in the deep.[2]

ENDURING THE STORMS

One of the many things I so appreciate about the Lord's dealings with His children is the fact that He moves in a great calm. He truly is "slow to anger." And yet, it doesn't always seem to be the case from our perspective. In fact, there are times His chastening moves into our lives like a thunderstorm.

In the natural life, storms often arrive unannounced. Once it's there, the entire horizon is dark and menacing. The brilliant lightening bursts only accentuate the blackness of the sky. If the person didn't know better, it would seem as though that thunderstorm were there to stay forever; but experience tells him that it will only be a matter of a few hours before it moves out of the area.

The storms of adversity and affliction we face in life are this way. They tend to move into our lives for a period of time before dissipating into past memory. The truth is that there is an element of endurance involved in trials. As James said, "...let the process go on until that endurance is fully developed, and you will find you have become men of mature character..."

Trials can take on all kinds of different forms: a difficult boss, an unfaithful mate, a debilitating disease, the loss of a loved one and so on. Certainly one of the most challenging types of trials is persecution. This is what the believers of the Asian city of Smyrna faced during the days of the Early Church. Through the apostle John, Jesus sent them this message:

"I know of your tribulation and of your poverty —though in fact you are rich! I know how you are slandered by those who call themselves Jews, but in fact are no Jews but a synagogue of Satan. Have no

fear of what you will suffer. I tell you now that the
devil is going to cast some of your number into prison
where your faith will be tested and your distress will
last for ten days. Be faithful in the face of death and I
will give you the crown of life." (Revelation 2:9-10 PHP)

These dear people did suffer for their faith. One of their
number who was claimed by martyrdom was their beloved
bishop Polycarp. When he was hauled before the Roman
proconsul and ordered to renounce his faith, Polycarp answered,
"Eighty-six years have I served Him, and He has never done
me any harm. How could I blaspheme my King and Savior?"

In His message to these beleaguered saints, Jesus told them
that they would face ten days of imprisonment. Of course,
doing a ten-day jail stint wouldn't be that intimidating for most
people. I have talked to prisoners who have "been down" for
thirty years. But Jesus didn't mean that they would literally be
in jail for ten days. This is the typical figurative language found
throughout the book of Revelation. Jesus used the number ten
because it is symbolic of completion. He was simply telling
these believers that they would enter a time of suffering which
would fully accomplish all that God intended for their lives.

The ten day period represents a season of time—and only
the Lord knows how long it will actually last. Of course, while
a person is in the midst of such a trial, he doesn't realize that
it will eventually come to an end. The uncertainty, confusion
and insecurity involved in facing physical or emotional pain all
combine to accomplish God's purposes in the person's life.

And the Lord understands that human beings typically
experience certain natural emotions through such a trial. During
the first phase of this period, the person feels stunned by the new
development. A certain kind of emotional numbness typically
sets in for awhile. As the shock wears off, he rallies his strength
and musters up a degree of hope that deliverance will soon
arrive. But alas, the suffering continues unabated. One dark day

follows another and his hope begins to wane. Eventually the person feels that all hope is gone. An overwhelming sense of futility overcomes any thoughts of deliverance. He has come to "the end of his rope" and lapses into helpless resignation. He has been pleading for God's help through the entire ordeal. But the tenth day represents the point—and only the Lord knows when this is actually reached—when the person has completely put his situation into God's hands. Only the passage of time can fully accomplish what must happen for the person.

One of the most difficult aspects of going through such a trial is that the Lord often seems to pull away right when the person most feels the need for His presence. He is there, of course, but for His own eternal purposes He often makes it seem as though He is far removed. Over and over again this is seen in the lamentations of the psalmists:

- "Why do You stand afar off, O Lord? Why do You hide Yourself in times of trouble?" (Psalm 10:1)
- "How long, O Lord? Will You forget me forever? How long will You hide Your face from me?" (Psalm 13:1)
- "O my God, I cry by day, but You do not answer; and by night, but I have no rest." (Psalm 22:2)

This aloofness is all part of God's strategy to deepen and strengthen a person's faith. It reminds me of a story David Ravenhill once shared at a Pure Life Ministries conference. An acquaintance had a dream one night where the Lord walked up to three different believers. He gave the first Christian a big, cheerful hug. He then moved on to the second person, giving him a friendly pat on the back. Finally, He walked by the third believer without even acknowledging him. "I guess you really love that first guy, Lord," the person said in his dream. The Lord explained that he was missing the point. He loved all three equally, but the first person was a baby

Christian who needed a lot of encouragement. The second Christian had a level of maturity which required no more than a pat on the back. The last person had faith that was deep enough to endure what seemed to be a snub. He knew his God well enough to know that the Lord had a good reason to pass him by.

One's natural inclination would be to think that the godliest saints live in a perpetual sea of God's love and attention. And, of course, such people do experience those times. But it has been my experience that those who have traveled the furthest in their spiritual journey are the ones who have been forced to get beyond the realm of feelings (i.e., *feeling* God's presence) and have learned to live a victorious Christian life on the sheer faith they have in God's good character.

My guess is that Oswald Chambers was one such person. He wrote, "I have to believe that God is good in spite of all that contradicts it in my experience."[3]

THE ETERNAL PURPOSE

Oftentimes trials seem more difficult than they actually are because eternity is so miniscule in the sufferer's mind. In fact, I would say that the more earthly-minded a Christian is in his daily life, the more painful his trials are going to feel. Likewise, the more eternally-minded a person is, the better equipped he will be to properly handle adversity.

Allow me to illustrate this with a silly story. As part of a very difficult trial that Kathy and I have recently faced, we were required to move three separate times.

During one of those trips—as I bounced down the highway in a rental truck—I complained to the Lord about the beating our furniture was taking through these moves. "Lord, it's killing me to see our stuff being banged up like this," I protested. "And I don't need to remind You that we're not in a financial position to run out and buy new furniture!"

For one split second, after registering that complaint, I saw those possessions (actually they represented the entire two-year trial in which we were engulfed) in light of eternity. It was as if I could look back on this segment of my timeline—a period that felt like a huge, meaningless waste of time—from the perspective of the hereafter. Now those pieces of furniture, that seemed so important to me at the time, meant nothing to me. From that vantage point, what stood out so significantly was how God used the losses we suffered to deepen our faith and better prepare us for life in another world. It was amazing how a momentary revelation could completely alter my value system.

Yes, trials typically involve the loss of something precious to us. It might be the loss of freedom, health, comfort, peace of mind, a coveted job, a friendship or even a loved one. But, for the submitted believer, the loss experienced in one world is the gain of the next. Actually, if we could really see how much we will one day value those eternal gains, the losses we suffered on earth to win them will seem like nothing in comparison. I think that was the point that Paul made when he told the Romans, "In my opinion whatever we may have to go through now is less than nothing compared with the magnificent future God has planned for us." (Romans 8:18 PHP)

*"Time is the dressing room
for eternity."* –Anonymous[1]

*"God hangs the great things
of eternity upon the small wires
of times and seasons in this world:
that may be done, or neglected in a day,
which may be the groundwork of joy
or sorrow to all eternity."*
–J. Flavel[2]

*"Exercise yourself spiritually, and
practice being a better Christian
because that will help you not only now
in this life, but in the next life too."*
–The Apostle Paul[3]

*"Our God is coming,
but not in silence; a raging fire
is in front of him, a furious storm
around him. He calls heaven and earth
as witnesses to see him judge his people."*
–The Psalmist[4]

Part Three:

THE ANTEROOM OF ETERNITY

"The godly man gives generously to the poor.
His good deeds will be an honor to him forever."
–The Apostle Paul[1]

"It is not the beat of the pendulum
or the tick of the clock that measure time,
but it is the deeds which we crowd into it."
–Alexander MacLaren[2]

BUILDING A GODLY TIMELINE

H enry Aaron was my hero when I was a young boy. This came about because I had played on a Little League team named the Braves. Of course his major league career was in full swing by the time I gave my heart to the Milwaukee Braves in the early 1960's.

Actually, the first spring training game Aaron played in as a Brave was on March 14, 1954, five days after I was born. I was only three-years-old when his MVP season led the team into the first of two consecutive World Series appearances. By the time "Hammerin' Hank" finished his 22-year career, he held the all-time baseball records in a number of categories. However, his most unforgettable moment surely must have been April 8, 1974 when he hit his 715th homerun, passing Babe Ruth's seemingly invincible record. As of the writing of this book, Henry Aaron is 76-years-old and can certainly look back over his baseball career with a true sense of satisfaction.

Another man who accomplished much during his time on earth was Spencer Tracy. He was born in 1900 and began his acting career thirty years later. By the time of his death in 1963—just after completing the filming of "Guess Who's

Coming to Dinner"—he had appeared in some 75 feature films. During that 33-year career, he amassed a record nine Academy Award nominations for Best Actor—winning twice. He too enjoyed an accomplished life.

I mention these two American icons to make a simple point: What these men achieved in their respective careers will one day dissolve into nothingness, while the highlights of your life as a Christian will stand brightly forever.

"Just what accomplishments are you referring to?" you might ask incredulously. "What have I ever done that could begin to compare to the historic legacy these men left behind?"

Well, what about that time you passionately shared your faith with your co-worker? The Lord used you to lead that person into a saving relationship with Jesus Christ. A thousand years from now, as you are witnessing the blessed existence of your friend's life in heaven—something he will still be thanking you for every time he sees you—do you really believe that Hank Aaron's 755 homeruns will be of any importance?

Look back on all of the many times you interceded for loved ones. Every one of those prayers has become a living memorial in the sacred halls above. Ten thousand years from now, do you really think Spencer Tracy's 75 movies will even begin to compare to that heritage?

And what about the time you were being ridiculed for your faith by that group of acquaintances and the Lord helped you to maintain a gracious demeanor in the midst of their verbal attack? Are you really of the opinion that one of those gold-plated statues Spencer Tracy left behind on planet earth can be considered superior to that display of courage?

Let's not forget the time that you endured that withering trial. In spite of your sufferings—so severe that they caused you to grapple with the question about whether or not God even exists—you came through that test with your faith intact and even strengthened. From an eternal perspective, how could any of Henry Aaron's baseball accomplishments measure up against that?

Those moments in your life that you probably have devalued are the stuff of legends in the hereafter. As far as I can tell, Spencer Tracy died an unrepentant alcoholic. When you think of earth life in terms of what is truly lasting, what did he *ever* do that was lasting? Perhaps that is what David was referring to when he said, "The Lord opposes those who do evil, that He may eradicate their memory from the earth." (Psalm 34:16 Har) Solomon took that thought even further when he said, "The memory of the righteous is blessed, but the name of the wicked will rot." (Proverbs 10:7)

The fact is that you are currently in the process of building something significant that will endure forever. I could even say that God has destined you for a life of great feats.

BUILDING YOUR TIMELINE

When you were enlisted into the army of God, you were assigned a specific task that only you could properly fulfill. Actually, your entire career has already been mapped out. I believe Horace Bushnell said it exactly right when he said, "God has a definite life-plan for every human person, girding him, visibly or invisibly, for some exact thing, which it will be the true significance and glory of his life to have accomplished."

Perhaps it was what the apostle Paul wrote that inspired Mr. Bushnell to write that: "God has made us what we are, and in our union with Christ Jesus he has created us for a life of good deeds, which he has already prepared for us to do." (Ephesians 2:10 GNB)

Let's go back to our screen star's career as an example. Most of Tracy's films were produced by Metro-Goldwyn-Mayer film studio. This is not the way it actually happened, but let's say that when Spencer Tracy was a young, promising actor, Louis Mayer took a liking to him and decided he was going to make him the studio's next star. The powerful mogul knew his production crew was preparing some motion pictures that would be surefire hits. So he simply told his producers that he wanted Tracy to get the lead role in each of those upcoming films. All the young actor had to do was to play the part that was already scripted for each movie and he was on his way to certain stardom.

I realize your situation seems much vaguer and perhaps more mundane than this example. Of course, the difference between us and Hollywood actors is that we walk by faith, not by sight, right? Even if I knew you personally, I probably couldn't tell you what path God has ordained for your life. What I know for certain is that you have one. It was mapped out long ago and you are the leading actor in it. "Like an open book, you watched me grow from conception to birth," said an amazed David. "All the stages of my life were spread out before you, the days of my life all prepared before I'd even lived one day." (Psalm 139:16 MSG) This is just as true of your life as it was of his!

In fact, I would go so far as to say that the following words could have been spoken directly to you: "Before I formed you in your mother's womb I chose you. Before you were born I set you apart. I appointed you to be a _____." (Jeremiah 1:5 NET)

Only you and the Lord can fill in that blank, but the answer to that vital question will not be arrived at cheaply. We are not just talking about how the rest of your life is going to play itself out: this appointment will also have significant ramifications upon your eternity. In other words, it is of extreme importance. Dwight Moody said, "Let us not talk of rest down here, we have all eternity to rest in. This is the place for *work*...Our works shall follow us. We shall leave a record behind us, if we are only faithful, ere the night comes. We can set streams running here in this dark world that shall flow on after we have gone to heaven."[3]

If you're not clear about your appointed work, I encourage you to do your utmost to discover it. God greatly desires to give you, at the very least, a sense about His direction for your life. In fact, it would be a source of joy for Him just to see that you are interested. If you want to find out what your place is in His kingdom, here are three things you can do.

First, begin a systematic prayer vigil over this question. You don't necessarily have to spend hours each day seeking God about it, but if you will make it a matter of daily prayer for the next month or so, I'm confident the Lord will give you a sense about what it is.

Second, ask yourself some pertinent questions: What are my spiritual gifts? What do I feel that I am most suited to do? What kind of ministry activities appeal to me? What am I passionate about? How does my personality fit in with what I sense God has for me? Try to be open to the possibility of the Lord using you in an unexpected manner. Remember: the point in this is to discover His will for your life, not to convince Him to bless your plans!

Third, has the Lord opened any doors for you to become involved in some type of ministry work? Be careful on this one because an open door does not necessarily mean it is God's will for you. Nevertheless, it can be an important clue that can help you solve the mystery.

Keep one more thing in mind as you set out to discover God's will for your life. The Lord usually only reveals one step at a time. In 1986 my life's work was laid out for me when the Lord burdened me to help men in sexual sin. The details about how it would actually play itself out remained a mystery to me for quite some time. I had to grope my way along the obscure path before me, but as I did, He opened the right doors.

Actually, some believers receive a variety of assignments during their spiritual career. Consider a typical soldier as an example. Upon completion of boot camp, Private Jones is assigned to Fort Drum in New York for specialized training. After several months there, he receives orders to report to the army depot in Corpus Christi, Texas, where he works as a logistics coordinator for the next two years. Then one day he receives a one-year assignment to Camp Arifjan in Kuwait. This type of moving around makes up the work history of his entire thirty year career.

The Lord handles people in different ways. Some will look back over their timelines and see how He had used them doing a variety of tasks in different locations. Others will remain planted at one task for their entire lives. Some people will be involved in an actual ministry while others will carry out godly duties in an unofficial capacity. Whatever the case may be, the important thing is that a person puts his heart into whatever assignment he has been called to perform.

The fact of the matter is that you have certain talents and gifts that the Lord desires to use in His kingdom. And yet, as important as the work is to His greater purposes, He is even more concerned about *you*. Therefore, His plan for your life will not only include your natural strengths, but it will also take into account your limitations. No matter what He has you doing, He wants you to be completely dependent upon Him all the way through the journey. Typically, the Lord puts His people into situations where they have to rely on Him to be able to succeed. Your weakness will actually allow Him to operate at His full capacity through your life: "...for power is perfected in weakness." (II Corinthians 12:9) Think of it— His power operating perfectly through your life!

God has mapped out a course for your life that takes into account every necessity. Imagine that you are an army sergeant who has been given orders to lead an expedition into the interior of Antarctica. Before departing, your commanding officer gives you a map and points out to you designated drop-off spots for supplies along the route. Those supplies will be there awaiting your arrival. It has all been strategized at army headquarters and you can be sure you will be well cared for. How much more true is that of the Lord's care for us: "He who calls you is utterly faithful and he will finish what he has set out to do." (I Thessalonians 5:24 PHP)

When he was on that fateful trip to Jerusalem where he would be arrested, Paul told the Ephesian elders, "I do not consider my life of any account as dear to myself, so that I may finish *my course* and the ministry which I received from the Lord Jesus…" (Acts 20:24) Later, when he was at the very end of his stay on earth, he told Timothy, "I have fought the good fight, I have finished *the course,* I have kept the faith. (II Timothy 4:7) Yes, Paul had a definite course to fulfill in his lifetime, but so do you!

In fact, I want to take this one step further. We have talked a lot about the Greek term *kairos.* We've already seen how it has the sense of being a God-ordained moment. But this term can also refer to a season in a person's life. Let me put it this way: part of the calling upon your life as a believer is to "run the race" or fulfill the course He has ordained for your life. Actually, your entire lifespan is one long *kairos.* It is a spiritual opportunity you dare not miss. If you don't fulfill your calling, not only will you suffer terrible eternal loss, but the lives of other people could very well be in danger. There are people who no one else can reach in the way that you can. If you won't allow God to use you to help them, who will?

Let me make the case this way. What would have happened to all of those little girls rescued from Indian brothels by Amy Carmichael if she had not fulfilled God's course for her life? How many Chinese souls would have been eternally lost if Hudson Taylor had shirked God's call on his life?

You will never know what is down the path God has ordained for you if you don't take those first steps of obedience. Let's join the psalmist who exclaimed, "I'll run the course you lay out for me if you'll just show me how." (Psalm 119:32 MSG)

HIGH POINTS ON THE TIMELINE

Let's return to our metaphor of the army expedition into Antarctica. Your commanding officer tells you to lead your team along the designated route to a certain location. Along the way you are supposed to take the time to note all signs of animal life, record weather conditions and describe in detail the various ice and rock formations you encounter. In other words, there are definite tasks you are expected to fulfill as opportunities present themselves.

It goes without saying that such a mission would be fraught with "dangers, toils and snares." Every day would hold the risk of encountering a terrible blizzard or a man-eating polar bear.* Nevertheless, you bravely push on each day knowing that your captain is counting on you to fulfill your duty.

How would your mission be affected if you allowed those potential dangers and difficulties to dominate your thinking to the point that avoiding them became more important than accomplishing your assignment? What if you impatiently pushed toward the destination, helping yourself to the generous supplies provided along the way, but didn't put your heart into gathering that data? Can you imagine the look on your captain's face if you arrived back at the base a month later with nothing to show for your mission but a few hastily scribbled observations on a notepad?

Yes, we are headed toward a definite destination in our time journey. It is our final day upon earth. As Hebrews says, "...each person is destined to die once and after that comes judgment." (Hebrews 9:27 NLT) Judgment for you and me means that the Captain is going to look over our records to see how much we accomplished during the journey He laid out for us.

There are many facets to our earth mission. We must conduct ourselves in a manner that is worthy of our Savior: resist sin, remain aloof from the world's influences, stay pressed into God, and so on. Every aspect of our lives will be scrutinized when we stand before Him.

But when I think about a person presenting his timeline to the Lord, what stands out to me is whether or not he capitalized on opportunities to exhibit God's love to those

---

* I realize there are no polar bears in the Antarctica, but somehow an Emperor penguin just wouldn't provide a very intimidating example for our story!

in need. This is the mission to which every believer has been called. Like the army trekker, we might not take advantage of every opportunity, but we will want the record of our deeds to clearly show that we truly cared about the mission.

For those who aren't accustomed to thinking this way, it can seem like a terrible inconvenience to have to take the time during life's journey to get involved in the lives of others. When we are in the midst of the difficulties of life, dealing with other people's issues can seem very insignificant. But when we stand before the Lord, all of the pressing concerns we encountered in life will appear miniscule compared to the importance of the attitude we held toward other people. This is the mission every believer has been sent to accomplish on planet earth.

Let's again return to the metaphor of our army sergeant. The attitude he has when he begins the expedition is probably going to determine its outcome. If he has a lousy attitude, the outcome of his work will be pathetic. If he has a good attitude, he will put his heart into what he is doing. In other words, he will expend the time and effort to accomplish the duties he has been assigned—regardless of the difficulty involved.

What about the Christian who begins with a bad attitude—who wants the benefits of Christianity but doesn't want to give of himself? He can still mend his ways in the midst of the mission simply by changing his attitude toward it.

An attitude is similar to a river in that it has a flow to it. It is difficult for a person who is in the habit of regularly putting himself first to suddenly start thinking about others. In a sense, he must step out of the flow of selfish living and step into the flow of God's love. As he does so, it will become increasingly easier and even enjoyable to live that way. In other words, if the sergeant came to grips with the fact that he hadn't been putting his heart into his duties and simply began taking the time to collect the data he was sent to acquire, he would find that a whole new attitude would emerge within him.

One of the basic dynamics of Christianity that I fear few

really understand is that God's love begets more love. What I mean by that statement is that when a believer begins to extend himself to others he enters into a mysterious flow of life. To live one's life for oneself creates a deadness of soul. The more a person lives within the tiny confines of his own comfort zone, the stingier he will become with his time and money. He will have little or no desire to help anyone. Eventually he will become a spiritual Scrooge of sorts, a miserable old man who has nothing of value to show for his life.

On the other hand, the more a person can "get out of himself" and extend himself to others, the more he will *want* to do. The believer becomes a vessel of God's love by becoming involved in the lives of others. Paul stressed this to his two favorite protégés. He told Timothy that he should "have a reputation for good works..." (I Timothy 5:10) and should be "be rich in good works..." (I Timothy 6:18) He told Titus to "be zealous for good deeds" (Titus 2:14), to "be ready for every good deed..." (Titus 3:1) and finally, "learn to engage in good deeds to meet pressing needs..." (Titus 3:14)

He knew from much experience that there was something greater at stake than what others would receive from their exhibitions of kindness. Paul knew that the condition of the hearts of these two young men was at stake. As their timelines became populated with good deeds, their hearts would increasingly become filled with more of God's love.

In First Corinthians 15—where Paul talks at length about the resurrection of the believer—he concluded his teaching with a call to action: "Therefore, my beloved brethren, be steadfast, immovable, always abounding in the work of the Lord, knowing that your toil is not in vain in the Lord." (I Corinthians 15:58) This verse bears looking at in various paraphrases:

- ...busy yourselves in the Lord's work. Be sure that nothing you do for him is ever lost or ever wasted. (PHP)

- ...doing your full share continually in the task the Lord has given you, since you know that your labor in the Lord's service cannot be spent in vain. (Knox)
- ...work without limit, since you know that in the Lord your labor cannot be lost. (NEB)

Earlier I mentioned how important our little acts of kindness will prove to be in the hereafter. Each good deed that we did in our daily life here will take on enormous proportions when our lives are examined by the Lord.

One of the challenges we face in life is that our memories are so untrustworthy. We usually forget all about our thoughtful deeds within days—or even minutes—of doing them. This is partially so because we tend to see them as being insignificant.

However, the Lord doesn't view them in the same light. Actually, He doesn't overlook or forget *any* of our good deeds. Every time you smiled at someone who needed to experience human warmth, or helped an elderly woman with her groceries, or watched the neighbor's children, or stopped by the nursing home to read Scripture to some lonely soul, or sent an offering to a missionary or whatever else you might have done...Every single good deed you have ever committed has been properly noted in heaven's annals.

Nehemiah seemed to understand this. Four different times in his short narrative he implored God to remember the good things he had done. He really didn't need to be concerned because, in some inexplicable way, God has a memory bank where all our good deeds are safely stored. (see Hebrews 6:10)

Isn't this what Jesus was referring to when He counseled us not to bother storing up treasure on earth but to make our deposit in the eternal realm? (Matthew 6:19) Let's conclude this chapter by meditating on this great truth as it is provided through the following paraphrases:

- "Store them in heaven where they will never lose their value..." (LB)
- "But gather and heap up and store for yourselves treasures in heaven..." (Amp)
- "But amass wealth for yourselves in Heaven..." (WNT)

Yes, heaven is your destination and won't it be nice to have a rich "bank account" awaiting your arrival? Won't it be wonderful to hear the Lord expressing His gratitude to you for the way you lived your life? "And as we live with Christ, our love grows more perfect and complete; so we will not be ashamed and embarrassed at the day of judgment, but can face him with confidence and joy..." (I John 4:17 LB)

*"We've traveled too far, and our momentum
has taken over; we move idly towards eternity,
without possibility of reprieve or hope or explanation."*
–Tom Stoppard[1]

*"I've been out of step with you for a long time...
God, make a fresh start in me, shape a Genesis week
from the chaos of my life. Bring me back from gray exile,
put a fresh wind in my sails!"*
–David[2]

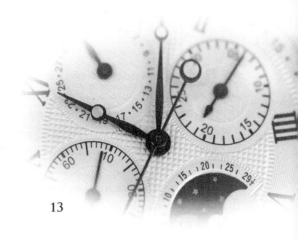

GAINING MOMENTUM TOWARD ETERNITY

After several disappointing seasons, the Oakland Raiders thought their fortunes were about to change when they were awarded the very first pick of the 2007 NFL draft. This is an annual event when the best college football players are scooped up by professional football teams in need of fresh athletes.

After months of anticipation in the football world, the day finally arrived. The commissioner stepped up to the podium to announce the number one pick of the draft. "The Oakland Raiders pick JaMarcus Russell from Louisiana State," he proclaimed grandly.

Nearly every football pundit thought picking the young quarterback was a great choice. ESPN's Mel Kiper predicted that Russell would "immediately energize" the Raiders' entire franchise. He also thought it was possible that within three years he could be "one of the elite top five quarterbacks in the league."

There were plenty of reasons for all the optimistic hype. Russell's abilities and arm strength were considered to be "off the charts" for a quarterback. Everyone agreed his potential was enormous.

During his stellar college career, JaMarcus Russell had led LSU to 25 wins against only four losses. His thrilling Sugar Bowl victory over Notre Dame should have propelled him into a successful career in the NFL. As a talented star quarterback, he was expected to provide dynamic leadership to his new team.

Unfortunately, things started to sour immediately. Rather than accept the generous contract the Raiders offered, he refused to show up at training camp unless he received more money. The negotiations drug on for several months before he finally agreed to accept a contract that would pay him $68 million over six years. By the time he entered his rookie year, it was too late to properly prepare himself for his first season.

The following two years proved to be just as disastrous. Both years JaMarcus showed up at training camp physically out of shape. He began developing a reputation for binge eating and having a halfhearted commitment to winning. There were also rumors that he was abusing codeine-enhanced cough syrup. One of his teammates saw him nodding out during a team meeting and asked himself, "Is that the guy who's going to lead us?" Someone else said, "It wasn't that Russell was a divisive presence in the Raiders' locker room. He was just there, sucking the life out of the room with his lack of work ethic, desire and inspiration."

At the end of the 2009 season, JaMarcus was finally released. A blog entry from a fan sums up the results of the young man's short career: "For the rest of his life he has to live with the label of being the biggest NFL bust of all time and that's how people will always remember him. All the money in the world cannot erase it either."

How did this young man go from being one of the most gifted, budding quarterbacks college football has ever produced to being considered "the biggest NFL bust of all time?" He began his career making one poor choice after another until he found himself sliding down a slippery slope from which he couldn't recover.

His story also provides a fitting illustration of a spiritual principle that plays a very important part in our journey toward the hereafter. The apostle Paul shares this unavoidable law of the kingdom of God:

> Don't be under any illusion: you cannot make a fool of God! A man's harvest in life will depend entirely on what he sows. If he sows for his own lower nature his harvest will be the decay and death of his own nature. But if he sows for the Spirit he will reap the harvest of everlasting life by that Spirit. Let us not grow tired of doing good, for, unless we throw in our hand, the ultimate harvest is assured. Let us then do good to all men as opportunity offers, especially to those who belong to the Christian household. (Galatians 6:7-10 PHP)

The fact of the matter is that we are constantly living in the fruit of yesterday's sowing. Likewise, today's lifestyle is setting the stage for the conditions we will face tomorrow.

Paul employed a metaphor in this passage that an agricultural community would easily recognize. Those who have been around farming operations understand that Nature operates under certain strict guidelines. For instance, if a person buys cheap grass seed, or even sows good grass seed sparingly, he will end up with an unhealthy lawn prone to a takeover by weeds.

Paul said that this dynamic also applies to our behavior. Each thought, word and action carries with it a germ that will come to life later. This is a basic formula of life. It doesn't mean that God doesn't love a person because He allows the person has to face the consequences of his actions. There is nothing arbitrary about it. It is simply the law of causation at work. In spite of the fact that Paul began by saying, "Don't be under any illusion...," there are those people who are determined to believe that they can flout this law under the guise of grace.

One of the reasons some people ignore this spiritual principle is that the harvest for one's actions often doesn't come into fruition until much later. They reason that since the bad crop is delayed there won't be one.

Actually, the spiritual law Paul presented that day was simply a new way to express what Moses had told the Hebrews some 1,200 years before: "...if you diligently obey the Lord your God, being careful to do all His commandments which I command you today, all these blessings will come upon you and overtake you...But if you do not obey the Lord your God...all these curses will come upon you and overtake you." (Deuteronomy 28:1-2, 15-16) And so it is that people have blessings or curses following them all the days of their lives.

LIVING IN DEFEAT

There is a form of Christianity that is incredibly dull and meaningless. It is the lukewarm mentality that Jesus found so nauseating with the Laodicean Church. It is the person who is neither on fire for God nor utterly given over to the devil.

It was this kind of lethargy that destroyed the career of JaMarcus Russell. He wanted the pay and glory of being an NFL player without putting forth the effort. His outstanding feature was his lazy, defeatist attitude. He never gave any indication that he saw himself leading his team into a winning season. He was content to float along with the vague hope that somehow things would improve. When a person is stuck in this type of rut, every effort he puts forth seems like an enormous taxing of his strength.

Halfhearted Christians don't typically entertain a proper perspective of their lives. In their minds, every effort takes on exaggerated proportions. If they could only take a seat in the grandstands and view themselves from Another's perspective, they would see that for every step they have taken toward God, they have taken a couple of steps backward.

They sow a seed or two in the Spirit and wonder why their efforts produce so little. What they don't understand is that for every healthy seed of corn they have planted, they have thrown a handful of thistle seeds into the garden of their lives. The cornstalks may be real, but they have become overwhelmed with weeds! No wonder they feel so hopeless!

One of the reasons such Christians remain stuck is they have never experienced Christianity on a level any higher than what they currently live. They flatter themselves that they are walking in the Spirit, but when a godly saint begins to explain what that life is actually like, a blank look comes across their faces.

Life in the spiritual realm very much moves by the force of momentum. When a person walks in the flesh, he tends to become buried by carnal thinking and an infatuation with worldly allurements. The law of sowing and reaping dictates that a defeated person is going to continually be setting himself up for more defeat the next day. Every time a person gives over to some worldly temptation, it smooths the way for the next. Before one knows it, he is in a freefall down the side of that mountain and he cannot seem to slow his momentum.

I touched on this dynamic once in a sermon about the Apostasy—the great falling away from God predicted in Scripture for much of the end-times Church. As part of that message, I offered the audience the following self-examination. I invite you to take a seat in the grandstands and try to take an objective viewpoint of your own spiritually.

MOMENTUM TEST

Anytime a person physically falls, gravity acts as a force which drives the person to the ground. Once set in motion, this momentum is not easily reversed.

So it is with the "Great Falling Away" predicted for the Last Days.* Scripture gives every indication that many professing Christians will move in increasing velocity away from the things of God and toward the things of the world. The closer we come to the end, the more difficult it will be to swim against this powerful current.

The following list is provided to allow people to examine which direction their ongoing lifestyles are taking them:

19 SIGNS YOU ARE BECOMING A PART OF THE GREAT APOSTASY:

1. Prayer is either nonexistent or mechanical
2. You know the Word but you don't really live it
3. Earnest thoughts about eternal matters no longer grip your heart
4. You can indulge in inward and outward sin without feeling devastated
5. A longing for holiness is no longer a predominant passion of your life
6. The pursuit of money and possessions are an important part of your life
7. You can sing worship songs without really meaning what they express
8. You can hear people treating eternal issues flippantly without becoming upset
9. Your main concerns are of your temporal, earthly life
10. Conflicts in your relationships with others are not a major concern to you
11. You no longer hunger for a deeper life in God
12. You don't live with a full and grateful heart

---

* See Matthew 24-25; II Thessalonians 2; II Timothy 3:1-4:4; II Peter 2-3; and Revelation 17-18.

13. You have little concern over and make little effort to meet the needs of others
14. You always see your level of spirituality in positive terms
15. You are more concerned about your pet doctrines than people's souls
16. Sports, entertainment and pleasure are important aspects of your life
17. You are more concerned with your image than with the reality of your life with God
18. You are full of bitterness, or criticism, or pride, or covetousness, or lust
19. You have a head full of knowledge and a heart made of stone.

If you find that a number of these signs are true of your life, I would suggest you write them down and take them into prayer every day for at least two weeks. Lay that sheet of paper out before God and ask Him to help you to change that particular characteristic of your life. You do not need to remain in this flow of life.

REVERSING THE MOMENTUM

Most Christians I know who have attempted to halt their spiritual declension have made a number of attempts to turn things around but quickly get discouraged and slide back into their old familiar ruts.

Let's face it, we have a carnal nature that is not interested in spiritual things, we are surrounded by a godless culture and we have a relentless foe that is attempting to destroy us. We simply do not have the power within ourselves to overcome such force. However, the power we have access to through the Almighty is more than enough to sustain a victorious lifestyle. No child of God should live in spiritual defeat.

The greatest resistance we face is not from the three opposing forces mentioned above. The greatest challenge to turning the tide of our lives from defeat to victory is perception. We must see the victory out ahead on our timeline, obligate ourselves to fighting for it and believe God to supply the means to achieve it.

This battle must begin with repentance—a turning away from carnality, worldliness and sin in favor of godliness. This requires a person to make a commitment to push toward the celestial kingdom and away from the kingdom of darkness.

This is another instance of needing to make Time our friend rather than our enemy. The reason people make New Year's resolutions is that it is a definite spot on the calendar they can use to launch their new commitment. In the months ahead, they know they will be able to look back to that significant day as the date they began their new behavior. There is a certain wisdom to this game plan (unless you want a change in life now and the New Year is months away!).

The answer is for the person to set his own date—say, the beginning of the next month, or perhaps an upcoming holiday. He should plan it a week or two in advance. That will give him time to pray about it and build anticipation. It is a good idea for such a person to tell his mate, pastor and close friends so that they too can be praying for his big day. Rather than spending his special day at home—with all its many distractions—he should do something creative like renting a cabin in a state park. He should spend at least eight hours involved in spiritual activities: fasting, studying the Bible, praying, listening to godly sermons or worship music and, most of all, asking the Lord to help turn things around in his life.

After the events of that day have concluded, he must begin his "new life" with a different lifestyle. Some habit patterns will have to change. Certain indulgences (too much television, Internet, etc.) will have to be discarded. New habits (i.e., a solid devotional life, getting involved in the lives of others, etc.) will need to be established. His special day won't mean anything if he simply returns to his old behavioral ruts.

In the weeks and months that follow, he will find himself pointing to this 24-hour period as a pinnacle in his history as a believer. It is the day he made a concrete commitment to live his Christian faith at a new level.

Now that the hold of the world has been largely broken, the believer can move forward with new confidence. In the same way that sowing to the flesh has reaped a destructive harvest in the past—keeping him bogged down in spiritual lethargy—he will find that sowing to the Spirit will exert the same force upon his life in a positive direction.

He will soon discover that his little efforts are being sown in clean and fertile soil. If he will bravely continue on in this new path, before he knows it he will begin to experience a marvelous harvest of godliness in his life. Paul promised, "But if he sows for the Spirit he will reap the harvest of everlasting life by that Spirit. Let us not grow tired of doing good, for, unless we throw in our hand, the ultimate harvest is assured."

There is an extremely important word hidden in these two sentences that we must examine: it is the word *life* (Gk. *zoe*). New Testament Greek offers two different words that we translate into English as *life*. In my book, *Intoxicated with Babylon*, I touch on the difference between these two terms:

> On another occasion, Jesus slightly altered the second statement: "He who loves his life (Greek, *psyche*) loses it; and he who hates his life *(psyche)* in this world *(kosmos)* shall keep it to life *(zoe)* eternal." (John 12:25) The deliberate choice of words for "life" sheds light on the real meaning. *Psyche* represents one's existence on earth, while *zoe* represents one's life in God. So Jesus was saying that whoever loves *his existence on earth* loses it; and he who hates *his existence in kosmos* shall keep it to *a life in God* forevermore." (Emphasis in original.)[3]

In short, *zoe* describes the energizing, invigorating force that empowers a dead soul with the very life of God. This explains why Jesus was called "the Prince of *Zoe*." (Acts 3:15) He also made the following statements about Himself:

- "I am the way, the truth and the *Zoe* (the life of God)."
- "I am the resurrection and the *Zoe* (the life of God)."
- "I am the Bread of *Zoe* (the life of God)."

He also said, "The thief comes only to steal and kill and destroy; I came that they may have *zoe* (the life of God) and have it abundantly." (John 10:10) If a Christian will sow into the Spirit, he will find God infusing him with power, vitality and new momentum.

So, when Paul promises us that if a person sows to "the Spirit he will reap the harvest of everlasting life by that Spirit," he is saying that every effort to pursue the things of God will reap a harvest of the spiritual vitality that comes from the very being of God. In other words, the believer can tap into the same kind of vitality that will one day be his in heaven. (see Hebrews 6:4-5)

As already mentioned, sowing and reaping are farming terms. One thing that stands out about this process of Nature is that it occurs over time. It would be utterly ridiculous for a farmer to throw a seed in the ground and expect a fully grown plant to be awaiting him the following morning. But how many Christians get discouraged and return back to their carnal ruts because they don't receive the blessing immediately? No! It takes time before the blessings begin to flow. "...if you diligently obey the Lord your God...all these blessings will come upon you and overtake you."

It should also be noted that the context of Paul's statement about sowing and reaping is that of doing good deeds toward other people. Of course, the greatest thing we can do for another person is to pray for him. There is no spiritual or natural activity we can do that is a more powerful and effective use of time than prayer. Yet, how many times have we prayed over some situation and then went on about our business and forgotten we had even prayed about it? I suspect most of our prayers are like that.

As an illustration of this, imagine a man with ten acres which he wants to fill with groundcover. He knows that if he can just get the seed into the ground, the forces of nature will take care of the rest. So he begins the project by spreading seed over the acre of ground in the northwest corner of his property. After completing the task, he busies himself with other projects and forgets about it. A few months later he happens upon that section of his property and is amazed to find his crop has already begun to sprout up and spread out.

The spiritual dynamic involved with offering effective prayers is much the same. We may pray over some situation and forget all about our prayer, but those prayers are not forgotten by Heaven. Not only do they allow the Holy Spirit to operate in that particular situation, but they birth a life of their own, so to speak. When groundcover is planted, it eventually goes to seed. New plants emerge and before long the entire area is covered in it. That's the momentum of Nature. We're all too accustomed to seeing it in operation in the weeds of carnality, but what a blessing it is to see that process reaping souls. Yes, "some a hundredfold, some sixty, and some thirty." Eternal fruit in the lives of others! And yes, rich and full blessings for one's own life!

Let us always remember that we are headed toward an eternal destination. The little things we do on earth will be of enormous importance to us in the hereafter.

Rather than allowing ourselves to drift out into the sea of worldliness—and perhaps even allow our faith to become shipwrecked before it makes it into that safe harbor beyond—let us fight to shift the spiritual momentum in our lives and make our heading a straight course for heaven.

As a fitting conclusion to this chapter, allow me to offer the following remarkable story that effectively illustrates momentum:

It happened that a ship was being towed across the Niagara River, in America, some little distance above the well known falls. Just as she got into the middle of the stream the hawser parted, and the unfortunate ship began to drift down the river, stern foremost. Efforts were made to save her from impending ruin, but every effort failed, and the unfortunate ship kept drifting further and further down the stream towards the terrible abyss below.

The news of the disaster spread along the banks of the river, and in a very short time there were hundreds of people, and they soon swelled to thousands, looking on in breathless anxiety to see what was to become of this unfortunate crew. There is a point that stretches into the river, which bears the name of 'Past Redemption Point,' and it is believed in the neighborhood that nothing that passes that point can escape destruction. The current there becomes so strong, the influence so fatal, that whatever goes by Past Redemption Point is inevitably lost.

The excited multitude upon the banks of the river watched the helpless ship drifting down farther and further, till she was within a few hundred yards of the fatal point. One after another were efforts made, but of no avail; still she drifted on. Only a few moments, and she passed the point. There was a kind of sigh of horror from the vast multitude as they saw that she had passed, for they knew she was lost.

But just as they rounded the point the captain felt a strong breeze smite upon his cheek. Quick as thought, he shouted at the top of his voice, 'All sails set!' and in almost less time than it takes to tell, every stitch of canvas on board the ship was stretched to catch the favoring gale. A cheer broke from the multitude on shore as they witnessed this last effort for salvation. But would it succeed?

The ship was still drifting, though the wind was blowing against it, and she was still moving downwards, stern foremost, though the wind was bulging out all her sails. It was a battle between the wind and the current. With breathless anxiety they watched the result. She slacks! Another moment—they scarcely dare whisper it—she stands! Yes, that terrible, downward course was actually stopped. There she was, still as a log upon the water. Another moment, and inch by inch she began to forge her way up the stream, until the motion was perceptible to those on shore, and one great shout of victory burst forth from a thousand voices, 'Thank God, she is saved! Thank God, she is saved!'

In a few moments more, with considerable headway upon her, she swept right up the stream, by Past Redemption Point, right into the still water, saved from what appeared to be inevitable destruction, just because in the very moment of moments she caught the favoring breeze."[4]

*"The great Day of Judgment determines nothing.
It only makes visible and palpable what we really are."*
–G. Calthrop[1]

*"May you always be filled with the
fruit of your salvation—the righteous character
produced in your life by Jesus Christ—for this
will bring much glory and praise to God."*
–The Apostle Paul[2]

ETERNAL WEIGHT OF GLORY

I t is very difficult for subjective humans to think about
eternity without wondering what is in it for themselves.
Well, there is certainly plenty in it for us, as we'll discover
through the rest of the book. After all, God is extremely big-
hearted and it is simply impossible to out-give Him.

However, there is a bigger issue involved with our redemption
and transformation than simply receiving rewards and eternal
bliss. When it's all said and done, the most important thing will
be whether or not the person's life brought glory to the Lord.

In the English language, the word "glorify" means to honor
someone in such a way as to encourage others to see that
person in the most favorable light. Surely the greatest thing the
world needs today is to be given an accurate representation of
God's character.

In First Samuel 2:30 the Lord laid down another one of
those unavoidable spiritual laws that govern life. He said,
"Those who honor (Heb. *kebed*) Me I will honor (*kebed*), and
those who despise Me will be lightly esteemed."

The literal meaning of this word *kebed* is "to be heavy," but
it is rarely employed in that context. It is almost always used in

Scripture regarding someone's honor, or even glory. But when you think about it, what is honor if it isn't weightiness?

When earth time has concluded and the masses of humanity are summoned to appear before the Almighty, the reality about the way they lived their lives will reveal whether they are "sheep" or "goats." They either honored God by their lives or they treated Him with indifference. Scripture makes it clear that there is no middle ground. It would be worthwhile to take a look at these two groups.

Let us first consider those who "despise" the Lord. At first glance, one would assume this refers only to the outright godless—to those who live in complete rebellion to God's authority. But the word despise (Heb. *bazah*) simply means to think lightly of or to consider someone as having little value. This describes the flippant attitude the mocker has about God and His kingdom. This person has shut off the conviction of the Holy Spirit and disdains the Lord's commandments. Paul asked some of the outwardly religious people of his day, "Do you think so lightly of his wealth of kindness, forbearance, and patience, and fail to see that God's kindness ought to induce you to repent? But in your obstinacy and impenitence you are storing up wrath for yourself on the Day of Wrath, when the justice of God will burst forth." (Romans 2:4-5 GSPD)

The picture presented by Paul's statement is that of a person who, over many years, has resisted every attempt by the Lord to reach his stubborn heart. Each time he has ignored God's loving overtures, he has added to the terrible sentence of wrath that is being stored up against himself. In the same way that the godly "stores up for himself treasures in heaven," so too the impenitent sinner is allowed to build his own eternal retribution. Judgment Day is of little concern to such a person, but nevertheless, one day he will face the outcome of his actions.

One of the aspects of the sinner's fate is the condition of his soul. Sin has a way of hollowing out a person. As the lust for sin takes over within, everything good and meaningful dissipates. God says that such people will be "lightly esteemed," or perhaps it could be said that their souls will become increasingly depleted. The psalmist said that they "are like chaff which the wind drives away." (Psalm 1:4) "They vanish," adds David, "like smoke they vanish away." (Psalms 37:20)[*]

As Mr. Calthrop (quoted above) points out, the great White Throne Judgment isn't so much about evaluating all of a person's deeds as much as it is exhibiting the reality of his character.[†] For a person to dishonor God by his life means that he has removed from himself the one Source who could have built into him the weightiness of a godly character that would survive the Great Judgment. He has proven himself foolish in the greatest issue of life. Spiritually speaking, he would be considered a lightweight. In one sense, his judgment is simply to spend eternity with the one he has proven to love more than all others: himself. What a terribly empty existence!

GODLY CHARACTER

By contrast, those who "honor" the Lord by properly reflecting His character to the world around them, will, in turn, be honored themselves. The Lord was literally saying that He will add weighty substance to their being. They will become increasingly more solid, more substantial.

As followers of Christ, we have a commission to vindicate the character of God by the way we live our lives. Jesus said, "Your light must shine so brightly before men that they can see your good works, and glorify your Father who is in heaven." (Matthew 5:16 Knox) Paul made the same point, wording it a little differently: "You have been bought, and at what a price! Therefore bring glory to God both in your body and your

---

[*] An interesting sidelight is found in C.S. Lewis's book, *The Great Divorce*, where he describes the inhabitants of hell as "ghosts," while the redeemed are characterized as "solid."

[†] The deeds of believers will be examined and rewarded at the Bema Seat Judgment, a subject we will examine more closely in the next chapter.

spirit, for they both belong to him." (I Corinthians 6:20 PHP) The way we do life either honors or dishonors His name.

Our behavior does affect God's reputation, but there is a deeper aspect to this dynamic than simply living an acceptable life in front of others. It is the work the Holy Spirit does within the heart and soul of people that is so important.

As the Lord is allowed to diminish a person's carnal nature, He is able to fill that void with His own character. Think of the love for people Jesus constantly exhibited. Consider how selfless and courageous He was in all that He did. Jesus Christ continually showed concern for the eternal wellbeing of those around Him. That's the character the Holy Spirit seeks to build within the believer.

The formation of godly character within a person is an interesting phenomenon. Our actions reflect our true character, and yet, at the same time, the way we behave toward others is the very thing that builds godly character. There is a momentum involved in this process. The more we allow God's love to flow through us toward other people, the more we become transformed by that love.

And yet, it is also true that a person's thinking and behavior are by-products of his character. We have all heard the metaphor, "That's only the tip of the iceberg." It is understood that this statement means that what is seen in a person or a situation is a small part of something much bigger that remains hidden from view. An iceberg often looks like no more than a scrap of ice floating on the sea, while in reality something monstrous lurks under the surface of the water.

In the same way, the caliber of a person's character is often seen in the small things of life: an inadvertent comment, one's countenance, a flash of anger, a smile and so on. And, of course, it goes without saying that a person's conduct in secret—when no one is there to witness it—is a telltale sign of what he is really like. Those actions are a direct by-product of the person's character. Glenn Meldrum says,

The character of a person refers to one's nature, temperament or personality. It is the inner life that makes us what we are and defines our thoughts, speech, decisions, behaviors and relationships. The moral facet of character determines a person's view of right and wrong, good and evil. The emotional dimension centers upon the subjective—how we respond to people and situations, whether with love or hate, trust or fear. The spiritual element reflects our belief in God and how He works in our lives. The intellectual aspect of our character speaks of our worldview, how we think and what we believe.

The moral, emotional, spiritual and intellectual dimensions of our lives unite to form the entirety of our character—who we are when life is easy or difficult, when we enjoy prosperity or suffer adversity, when people are watching and when no one is watching.[3]

HUMILITY AND HONOR

There is an interesting dichotomy involved in character building. On the one hand, it could be said that a person's character is directly tied to his reputation—his name. A person is known for his character or the lack thereof. Yet, when the Lord is developing a godly character within a person, part of the process is to help him get to the place that he is not concerned about what others think of him. In fact, sometimes the Lord requires a follower to completely "die to" his reputation.[‡]

A person who obsesses over what people think about him usually begins to do things in an attempt to make himself look better. A prideful person will always find a way to exalt himself, but it is nearly always at the expense of someone else. In the

---

‡ Surely Jesus experienced this: "He was despised and forsaken of men…" (Isaiah 53:3)

long run, such behavior actually diminishes one's character and people's respect.

"Before destruction the heart of man is haughty," said Solomon. "But humility goes before honor (*kebed*)." (Proverbs 29:23) Solomon could have been considering the contrasting characters of Moses and Pharaoh, Jeremiah and King Zedekiah, or any number of other prophet-monarch contests found in Scripture.

Jesus put great emphasis upon this spiritual law in His teachings. He expressed it this way: "Everyone who exalts himself will be humbled, and he who humbles himself will be exalted." He made this statement to His disciples when the mother of James and John attempted to secure the most prominent positions in the kingdom for her sons. (Matthew 20:20-28) He repeated these words later when the disciples themselves argued about which of them was the greatest in the kingdom. (Luke 22:24-26) He said this to the Pharisees when He censored them for their love of the chief seats. (Matthew 23:6-12) He also made this statement when He contrasted the self-righteous Pharisee with the repentant publican at the Temple. (Luke 18:9-14) He again made this point regarding the value system of God's kingdom when He sat a child down next to Him one day and told His disciples, "Whoever then humbles himself as this child, he is the greatest in the kingdom of heaven." (Matthew 18:4) It is obvious that Peter and James came to recognize the significance of this spiritual law as they both included it in their epistles many years later. (James 4:10; I Peter 5:6)

The people who are considered to be "high caliber" in the kingdom of heaven are those who have consistently humbled themselves before God and man. Such people are usually characterized with terms like decent, honest, upright and noble. That kind of solid character always brings glory to the Lord.

GOD'S TESTING FIRE

Have you ever noticed that the godliest people are typically those who have undergone tremendous trials in life? Moses chose rather "to endure ill-treatment with the people of God than to enjoy the passing pleasures of sin." (Hebrews 11:25) During his entire time of ministry, Jeremiah had to live with the accusation that he was a traitor to his country. As a teenager Daniel was torn from his family and marched into a foreign country as a captive. John the Baptist lived a tedious life in the sparse wastelands of the Judean desert for a number of years to prepare him for a few months of ministry.

Yet, there is one characteristic that each of these men held in common. They had the moral strength to confront the most powerful men of their age—and they did it regardless of the cost to themselves. The kind of virtue and solidness of character required to do this did not come about because they were privy to a good gene pool or because they were rich in self-esteem. Only the Almighty can forge this kind of character within a man.

The kingdom of God has different levels of spiritual authority that are established by the Holy Spirit's work inside of a person. Those who humble themselves before God, submit to His process of correction, obey Him from the heart, strive to grow closer to Him and allow Him to live His life through them, enjoy a privileged position in God's kingdom.§

The Lord has established a process to accomplish this spiritual authority and it can be seen in an important Greek term (and its derivatives): *dokime.* To help Timothy decide who should be given positions of leadership in the different churches he was overseeing, Paul told him, "Before they are asked to be deacons, they should be given other jobs in the church as a test (Gk. *dokimazo*) of their character and ability, and if they do well, then they may be chosen as deacons." (I Timothy 3:10 LB)

There are two important principles revealed here. First,

---

§ This position of "favor" can be seen throughout Scripture: Numbers 12:6-8; Daniel 10:11; Matthew 17:1; James 2:23; etc.

as the Living Bible brings out, it is simply wise to see how a person fares in a lesser role before promoting him into a more prominent position. Secondly, as the person operates in the functions of that lesser role, he will be certain to face difficult problems that will cause him to mature. This maturing process takes time, of course. As a friend of mine once said, "God can change a man in an instant, but it takes time to build character."

Paul told the Romans, "We can rejoice, too, when we run into problems and trials for we know that they are good for us—they help us learn to be patient. And patience develops strength of character (Gk. *dokime*) in us..." (Romans 5:3-4 LB)

The Lord allows the devil to test and tempt His children, but while the enemy does it in the hopes of destroying the person, God is allowing the process so that His son (or daughter) will grow stronger in his faith. The very thing that the harassing demon means for evil, God means for good. The comforting assurance believers have through all of this is that a sovereign God is overseeing the entire process. The enemy can go no further than He allows.

A perfect example of this occurred the night Jesus was arrested. Peter had been bragging about his willingness to follow Him all the way to death if necessary. It was then that Jesus told him, "Simon, Simon, behold, Satan has demanded permission to sift you like wheat." (Luke 22:31) Yes, the heavenly Father allowed the enemy to put Peter through a severe test that night, but that trial was kept within God's prescribed boundaries. It also later proved to bear much fruit in Simon Peter's life.

Some thirty years later, Peter wrote: "These trials are only to test (Gk. *dokimion*) your faith, to see whether or not it is strong and pure. It is being tested as fire tests (Gk. *dokimazo*) gold and purifies it—and your faith is far more precious to God than mere gold; so if your faith remains strong after being tried in the test tube of fiery trials, it will bring you much praise and glory and honor on the day of his return." (I Peter 1:7 LB)

For some inexplicable reason, our willingness to believe in the trustworthy character of God means everything to Him. Of course the Lord only employed the concept of precious metals to accommodate our earthly value system. If I were to paraphrase First Peter 1:7, it might sound something like this: "The fact that you believe in Me, to the point of entrusting your life to Me, means more than anything else in existence. The degree that you allow that faith in Me to be deepened through the rigors of earth life, is the amount of My glory you will share in the hereafter."

Now we have come full circle regarding God's great purpose for our lives. What is the point of it all? As we are humbled through various trials, temptations and afflictions, the Lord is building within us godly substance. It is this solid and weighty character that will bring the person "praise and glory and honor" in the age to come. A person of honor may lose all this world has to offer, but no one can rob him of the substance God has built within him. This is why the saints of old have been able to endure persecution and even martyrdom.

The apostle Paul probably understood this spiritual dynamic as well as anyone who has ever lived. He had visited "Paradise" in the "third heaven" (II Corinthians 12:2-4) and had a good sense about the operating principles there. He told the Romans, "Why, what we now suffer I count as nothing in comparison with the glory which is soon to be manifested in us." (Romans 8:18 WNT)

God is using all of the different circumstances of our existence on earth to build within us the kind of honorable character that we will enjoy forever. In the same way the ungodly will spend their eternity full of themselves, eating the fruit of their God-disdaining attitudes, we will forever reap inexpressible glories for the way we honored the Lord with our lives.

I will wrap up this chapter with a tremendous statement

Paul made to the believers in Corinth. (see II Corinthians 4:17) It warrants a look from several translations:

- These little troubles (which are really so transitory) are winning for us a permanent, glorious and solid reward out of all proportion to our pain. (PHP)
- Our troubles are slight and short-lived; and their outcome an eternal glory which outweighs them far. (NEB)
- The slight trouble of the passing hour results in a solid glory past all comparison. (Mof)
- For our light, momentary affliction (this slight distress of the passing hour) is ever more and more abundantly preparing and producing and achieving for us an everlasting weight of glory [*beyond all measure, excessively surpassing all comparisons and all calculations, a vast and transcendent glory and blessedness never to cease!*]. (Amp)

*"There are two days on my calendar—
'Today' and 'That Day.'"*
–Martin Luther[1]

*"Day by day the Lord observes the good deeds
done by godly men, and gives them eternal rewards."*
–David[2]

NUANCES AND ASPECTS OF BEMA

I t seems as though the life of a believer will be evaluated on the essence of his character—*who he is*—and also on the substance of his life—*what he has done.* I believe in God's perfect justice system that the woman who was bedridden for years—who allowed God to mold her into a greater resemblance of Jesus Christ—will be richly rewarded up yonder in spite of the fact that she did not have the ability nor opportunity to help other people. The essence of a person's character will play an enormous role in the determination of that person's quality of life in the hereafter.

However, there is simply no question that a person's actions will also be judged. (Matthew 16:27; Romans 2:6; Revelation 2:23; etc.) In the final analysis, earth life is a period of probation. It is where the mettle of our character is tested and we have the opportunity to make a difference in the lives of others. We are only given one opportunity to deny self and pick up our cross for the Savior; to resist the temptation to live for the pleasures of this world; to live a holy life for God. In other words, we have this one chance to do something worthwhile, something that will follow us into the hereafter.

What we do for God during our stay on earth will be of enormous consequence when we stand before Jesus Christ. This is the great Bema* Seat Judgment—the time when Jesus Christ will examine the timelines of believers in order to reward them for their good deeds. Jesus and Paul both touched on that momentous occasion:

"It's also like a man going off on an extended trip. He called his servants together and delegated responsibilities. To one he gave five thousand dollars, to another two thousand, to a third one thousand, depending on their abilities. Then he left...After a long absence, the master of those three servants came back and settled up with them." (Matthew 25:14-15, 19 MSG)

"But there are various kinds of materials that can be used to build on that foundation. Some use gold and silver and jewels; and some build with sticks and hay or even straw! There is going to come a time of testing at Christ's Judgment Day to see what kind of material each builder has used. Everyone's work will be put through the fire so that all can see whether or not it keeps its value, and what was really accomplished. Then every workman who has built on the foundation with the right materials, and whose work still stands, will get his pay. But if the house he has built burns up, he will have a great loss. He himself will be saved, but like a man escaping through a wall of flames." (I Corinthians 3:12-15 LB)

I have provided the two biblical passages above as a means of examining what it will be like when believers give an accounting to the Lord of their time on earth. While each of

* Bema is a Greek word describing the Roman tribunal used for adjudicating cases. Paul borrowed the term to describe the judgment of believers before Christ. (II Corinthians 5:10)

them offers valuable insights into that great Day, neither shows the entirety of the proceedings in itself. But by considering both together, I believe we can gain a fairly clear picture of what to expect.

The first thing that stands out about the Parable of the Talents is that the men standing before the Lord are His servants. Jesus obviously shared this story for the sake of His followers. In this particular case, the Lord offers three different examples: exceptional, average and minimal potential. He knows that all of us have different temperaments, abilities and personalities. He knows ahead of time just what each person is capable of handling. Five talents would be too much to ask of some, while two talents would be too little to ask of others.

God also takes into account the circumstances of our lives and the opportunities we have available to us to do something meaningful for His kingdom. The course He lays out for each of His servants—with all of its possibilities, temptations and challenges—is perfectly tailored to fit that person's abilities and potential. Above all else, He is merciful and just. He knows exactly what to expect of each of His children.

Those with exceptional promise—who faithfully discharge the duties given to them—will reap the greatest rewards. The one with average potential, who nonetheless was still faithful to his charge, will receive compensation in line with his efforts. Very little was expected from the third servant and with good reason; the Lord knew he wouldn't do anything with the little he had available. Is he an unfaithful servant who is to be cast into outer darkness or is he saved "through a wall of flames?" Only the Lord knows the answer to that question. One thing is for certain: the way we live our lives on earth will determine what we have to look forward to in the hereafter.

In succeeding chapters we will consider the pleasures of heaven which all will enjoy. Unfortunately, some people have the attitude, "I'll be satisfied just to make it to heaven." They want to believe that everything will be on identical footing there; that the land of enchantment will be equally enjoyable to all.

Do we really believe that could be true? Can we really imagine that someone who has shunned their cross in favor of a flowery path will enjoy heaven in the same way as someone like Jeremiah—who endured a difficult ministry for fifty years? Do we really think that the Judge of the Earth would be so unfair? Socialism—where every man receives the same compensation regardless of effort or ability—is a theory put into practice by certain governments on earth, but that faulty philosophy will find no place in God's kingdom.

We can rest in the fact that the Lord has access to every pertinent factor that has contributed to every thought we indulged, word we spoke and action we undertook. His justice will be absolutely perfect—down to the tiniest detail. All of it will be taken into account when He reviews our lives.

This brings up another faulty notion that can paralyze a believer's efforts on earth. Some people feel that anything they might do in life would be very insignificant in light of the ministerial accomplishments of some of the prominent Christian leaders who have ministered on earth.

My personal opinion is that many of those accomplishments that seem so huge from a worldly perspective are often overrated.

Let me offer a couple of personal experiences to illustrate this. In 1988, I appeared before millions of viewers on *The Oprah Winfrey Show* where God helped me to testify about how He had set me free of sexual addiction and transformed my life. From an outward perspective, that television appearance was probably the most significant single deed I ever accomplished during all my years of ministry.

By contrast, during a recent visit to Sacramento, Kathy and I visited an 80-year-old widow who had been a neighbor of mine when I was growing up. Nicki is not a believer; she's just a bored, lonely old lady. Her days are taken up with reading and watching television. We spent a couple of hours visiting with her before we had to leave. My last memory of her was her glowing smile of gratitude.

Perhaps that little gesture seems unimportant compared to a national television appearance, but I can assure you that it isn't viewed that way up yonder. That is the stuff that makes up heaven.

Allow me to offer another contrast. I'm thinking of certain gifted ministers who have enjoyed all the trappings and benefits of worldwide fame, only to have some habitual secret sin exposed for all to see. To me, the issue isn't so much the act of sin itself as much as the lack of godly character that allowed them to practice such blatant deeds of selfishness.[†]

In contradistinction to such men is Victor Plymire who left the United States in 1908 as a pioneer missionary to Tibet. Eleven years later he married a fellow missionary who gave birth to his son two years after that. The young couple found ministry in that closed country to be very difficult. Victor had been on the mission field for sixteen years before he had his first convert. In 1927, his son was struck down with smallpox. One week later, his wife also succumbed to the dread disease. He was refused permission to bury his loved ones in the local cemetery so he bought a small plot of land and dug their graves himself through the frozen ground. In spite of these devastating setbacks, Victor stayed at his post for many more years until the political instability of the area forced him into retirement.

Those men with international acclaim were able to preach the gospel to multitudes,[‡] while Plymire only ministered to a handful of people with very modest results.

---

† I am not referring to a man who has a godly track record but was setup by the enemy in a moment of weakness through some crafty temptation. We are all susceptible to such occasional failure.

‡ I do not mean to discredit the efforts of those who have been called by the Lord to minister through the media. There are many fine preachers who are faithfully discharging God's call upon their lives and will be rewarded accordingly.

I am using these extreme examples to make the point that the number of people a preacher ministers to is not necessarily as impressive to God as it is to us. Paul didn't speak of the size of the building that was constructed by a person's ministerial efforts but the quality of the materials that went into it.

One can only wonder about how many ministers have constructed enormous buildings with the faulty materials of pride and self-ambition. Year after year they have added to their edifices, their own success only furthering their delusion that they were doing it for the Lord. Perhaps by the time the undertakers have collected their bodies and the exaggerated eulogies have been administered over their caskets, they will have built enormous monuments to their time on earth. What a shock it will be for them on that great Day when they watch in horror as God's testing fire descends upon it leaving a measly pile of cinders!

There are two other significant issues that must be considered regarding the believer's judgment. The first is whether or not the work was done in and by the Holy Spirit. Solomon said, "Unless the Lord builds the house, they labor in vain who build it; unless the Lord guards the city, the watchman keeps awake in vain." (Psalm 127:1) Sentimental efforts will not be rewarded when we stand before Jesus Christ. We are first and foremost servants and we will be recompensed according to the degree we accomplished those duties we were assigned. (Luke 12:47; I John 2:17)

Another issue that is closely related is that of our motives. My guess is that when our deeds are examined one of the things that will stand out brightly (or perhaps glaringly) was why we did what we did. Was our heart really in what we were doing or were we doing it out of a reluctant obedience? Were we doing it to be seen by others or was it because we sincerely wanted to help someone?

Of course, only the Lord knows how to sort all of this

out. But we can rest assured that, in His system of justice, He will perfectly mete out rewards in line with a person's activities, motives and attitudes.

Be that as it may, we must accept the fact that there will be some who will be ashamed of their conduct on that great Day. (I John 2:28) Doesn't Scripture tell us plainly that some will lose their rewards?

- For if you love those who love you, what reward do you have? (Matthew 5:46)
- Beware of practicing your righteousness before men to be noticed by them; otherwise you have no reward with your Father who is in heaven. (Matthew 6:1)
- When you pray, you are not to be like the hypocrites; for they love to...be seen by men. Truly I say to you, they have their reward in full. (Matthew 6:5)
- Whenever you fast, do not put on a gloomy face as the hypocrites do, for they neglect their appearance so that they will be noticed by men when they are fasting. Truly I say to you, they have their reward in full. (Matthew 6:6)
- Watch yourselves, that you do not lose what we have accomplished, but that you may receive a full reward. (II John 1:8)

There will be those who had faith enough to secure salvation, but will have nothing else to show for their time on earth. One might shudder at the reality of Paul's words when he wrote that such a person would suffer "a great loss. He himself will be saved, but like a man escaping through a wall of flames."

As one minister described this person: "He will barely escape by the skin of his teeth, leaping out of a second-story window and running away for his life."[3] Another writer put it this way: "He is dragged through the smoke, saved by a hair's breadth, but sees all his toil lying there in white ashes at his feet. It is a grim picture."[4]

Beverly Carradine, a holiness preacher of a century ago, tells the story he heard of a man who had a vision of his judgment as he slept one night:

> There stood before him a shining being of such beauty of countenance, such dignity of bearing, such glory of appearance, that his soul almost swooned at the sight. In a little while the form began to fade away, and a voice said aloud, in his dream: "This would have been yourself, had you not turned aside from the will of God, and thus lost the grace that would thus have transformed you!"[5]

THE REWARDS

While there will be those who will have little to show for their time on earth, there will be far more who will enjoy the rewards granted them by a generous God.

Just think for a moment what it will be like when the Master reviews your life and, upon seeing all of the many good deeds you have done in His name, begins to lavish you with praise in front of all of the multitudes of heaven. (I Corinthians 4:5)

You will be astounded at God's memory. Every single time you resisted some temptation, you went out of your way to show kindness to someone, you gave of your sustenance toward God's work, you met some pressing need, you sacrificed your time and energy to help others—everything positive that you have done as a believer—is heralded before the ranks of heaven.

After a generous outpouring of love and appreciation, He will then say those immortal words: "Well done, my good and faithful servant...come and share the joy of your Lord." (Matthew 25:21 Knox)

Yes, "come and share" in the cheerful and joyous existence awaiting you in the great Land of Enchantment. You are about to step into an entirely new kind of living. In the final section, we will attempt to define "Beulah Land," but for now, we are faced with the question about what reward will be awaiting you.

Before we discuss the position of honor and responsibility your life has won you in the hereafter, we must take a temporary diversion. One of the components to life upon the New Earth will be that the corrupt governments that have reigned in the past will be overthrown once and for all. (Daniel 2:44)

Of course, it is the Messiah who will head up the new administration: "For a child will be born to us, a son will be given to us; and the government will rest on His shoulders; and His name will be called Wonderful Counselor, Mighty God, Eternal Father, Prince of Peace. There will be no end to the increase of His government or of peace, on the throne of David and over his kingdom, to establish it and to uphold it with justice and righteousness from then on and forevermore. The zeal of the Lord of hosts will accomplish this." (Isaiah 9:6-7) Randy Alcorn discusses this:

> The key word in Isaiah 9:7 is *increase*. Nearly every major English translation of the Bible renders the Hebrew word *marbiyth* as "increase" or "expansion." In other words, Christ's government of the New Earth and the new universe will be *ever-expanding...*
>
> It may be that Christ's government will always increase because he will continually create new worlds to govern (and, perhaps, new creatures to inhabit those new worlds). Or perhaps it will always increase because the new universe, though still finite, may be so vast that what Christ creates in a moment will never be exhaustively known by finite beings. From what we know of our current universe, with billions of galaxies

containing millions of billions of stars and untold planets, this is certainly possible. The restoration of the current universe alone will provide unimaginable territories for us to explore and establish dominion over to God's glory.[6]

This is a tremendous concept to consider. Rene Pache adds, "The future heaven is centered more on activity and expansion, serving Christ and reigning with Him…through the power and glory of resurrected bodies on a resurrected earth, free at last from sin and shame and all that would hinder both joy and achievement."[7] That is a slight glimpse of the future world to which we will belong.

But getting back to your judgment…After recounting your faithful service, the Lord will tell you, "Since you have been faithful over little things, I have great things to commit to your charge…" (Matthew 25:21 Knox) Actually, you will be appointed the overseer of five cities on the New Earth. (Luke 19:19)

Yes, a position in Christ's marvelous government has been reserved for you. (I Corinthians 6:2-3; Revelation 5:10) Little did you know at the time, but God was grooming you for this important position during your stay on earth. All that time you felt as though your little efforts didn't mean anything. You had a vague sense that the trials you endured were helping you spiritually, but you never could have guessed that they were preparing you for such a position of honor as this! And the salary you are to receive for your work is simply "out of this world!"

Not only does the Lord have a tremendous career mapped out for you—the kind of job you would have "died for" on earth—but He has also prepared for you a home perfectly suited to your taste. It too will be part of your reward "package."

Perhaps you will be one of those who would love the city life of New Jerusalem. Because of the unselfishness you exhibited on earth, you have been awarded a 5,000 square foot penthouse on the twentieth floor of a skyscraper in the heart of downtown. I realize that living anywhere in that marvelous city would be a blessing, but don't you think you would prefer a home like that over a simple two-bedroom apartment in the suburbs?

Maybe you are a nature loving person. What would it be like to find out upon your arrival that Jesus has constructed for you a sprawling ranch house located on 1,000 acres of lush terrain? Wouldn't that be better than a simple farmhouse on five acres?

Or perhaps you are one of those people who love to be near the ocean. Think how exciting it would be to find out that your eternal home will be built on a spectacular cliff overlooking the Great Sea! I'm sure you would be happy to have a small house a couple of blocks from the beach, but surely you can see that a home with a magnificent view would be preferable.§

Yes, living on the New Earth is going to be wonderful for every believer, but the quality of life we will enjoy there is being determined for us now. I think when it is all said and done, we will receive precisely what we have shown that we desired. Those who are content to live at a lower level of spiritual life on earth will receive that in heaven. Just as true is the fact that those who showed they greatly valued their eternal destiny will be awarded a quality of life reflecting that attitude.

God has granted to each of us the right to choose for ourselves the way we will live our lives in the next world. Let's go for the very best!

---

§ This is not as farfetched as it may seem. In Joshua 14:9, 14 we find Joshua and Caleb rewarded with sizeable portions of the Promised Land because they "followed the Lord my God fully." In Psalm 37, we are told that the humble (vs. 11) and the righteous (vs. 29) "will inherit the land." Nevertheless, whatever biblical precedent may or may not be applicable to these eternal scenarios, I suspect that the greatest aspect of the rewarding process will have more to do with our capacity to enjoy God's presence and to reflect His glory than any such outward gifts.

*"[In heaven] there was
no measurement of time
as we measure it here,
although many still spoke
in the old-time language
of 'months' and 'days' and 'years.'
I have no way of describing it
as it seemed to me then.
There were periods, and allotted times;
there were hours for happy duties,
hours for joyful pleasures,
and hours for holy praise.
I only know it was all harmony,
all joy, all peace, at all times
and in all conditions."*

—Rebecca Springer[1]

Part Four:

THE GREAT REALM OF ETERNITY

"Bless the Lord, the God of Israel,
who exists from everlasting ages past—
and on into everlasting eternity ahead.
Amen and amen!"–David[1]

"Eternity with all its years,
Stands present in Thy view;
To Thee there's nothing old appears;
Great God, there's nothing new."
–Isaac Watts[2]

ETERNAL GOD

The everlasting nature of the hereafter can only be understood in light of the great Eternal God who contains it. To pursue such knowledge (how can the finite mind really grasp the infinite?), we must turn to men who have had the most direct contact with God.

A number of biblical characters had personal encounters with God, but there is one man who stands out above the rest. The Lord said, "If there is a prophet among you, I, the Lord, shall make Myself known to him in a vision. I shall speak with him in a dream. Not so, with My servant Moses, He is faithful in all My household; with him I speak mouth to mouth, even openly, and not in dark sayings, and he beholds the form of the Lord." (Numbers 12:6-8)

The first recorded encounter that occurred between God and Moses was when the Lord revealed Himself as the great "I Am" in the burning bush. Who among us can conceive the depth of the revelation about God's essence Moses received that day? And what was it like to stand before Sinai, when "there were thunder and lightning flashes and a thick cloud upon the mountain?" (Exodus 19:16) Who can comprehend how

Moses was affected when he spent forty days in the very cloud of Glory on the mountaintop? I suppose if there has ever been a mortal who could have some sense of the immortality of God, it would be Moses.

The fact that the old lawgiver left behind only one psalm (Psalm 90) gives it added significance. What stands out about it are the numerous references he makes to time:

> Lord, through all the generations you have been our home! Before the mountains were created, before the earth was formed, you are God without beginning or end. You speak, and man turns back to dust. A thousand years are but as yesterday to you! They are like a single hour! We glide along the tides of time as swiftly as a racing river and vanish as quickly as a dream. We are like grass that is green in the morning but mowed down and withered before the evening shadows fall. (Psalm 90:1-6 LB)

This handful of statements by Moses offers priceless insight about God, man and time. As we will see, while man has an immortal soul and will live forever, eternity for him is something far different than it is for the Lord.

GOD: WITHOUT BEGINNING OR END

Moses tells us that God was "without beginning or end," or, as the NASB puts it, "from everlasting to everlasting." If we were to divide Eternity into sections, I suppose we could label them "Eternity Past" and "Eternity Future." "From everlasting" would thus represent Eternity Past, while "to everlasting" would represent Eternity Future.[3]

God alone has no beginning. Venture as far back as your mind can take you and you will find that God is there and beyond. Everything that has been created has a birth date;

God alone has existed from "Eternity Past." Imagine millions of years in the future and God is already there—and beyond. A.W. Tozer said it this way:

> "From everlasting to everlasting, thou art God," said Moses in the Spirit. "From the vanishing point to the vanishing point" would be another way to say it quite in keeping with the words as Moses used them. The mind looks backward in time till the dim past vanishes, then turns and looks into the future till thought and imagination collapse from exhaustion; and God is at both points, unaffected by either.
>
> Time marks the beginning of created existence, and because God never began to exist it can have no application to Him. "Began" is a time-word, and can have no personal meaning for the high and lofty One that inhabiteth eternity.[4]

When we consider the existence of God, we must take our thinking beyond the boundaries our finite minds tend to erect. Past (He existed), present (He exists) and future (He will exist) are one and the same to the Lord. Man will live forever, but it will be within the confines of time. God alone dwells outside of Time in the realm of eternal existence.[*]

From the Lord's vantage point, the entire region of Time is spread out before Him like a filmstrip on an editor's bench. He simultaneously looks upon every incident in our lives. In fact, He views the entirety of history in one glance. In other words, at one and the same moment He sees the multitudes perishing

---

[*] Time in heaven will most likely take on a different form than earth-time. There are two primary reasons I believe that it will exist in the hereafter. First, it is implied in different passages of Scripture. For instance, in Revelation 6:10, we find martyrs asking the Lord, "How long, O Lord, holy and true, will You refrain from judging and avenging our blood on those who dwell on the earth?" This is a clear indication of time. Second, and perhaps more importantly, is the fact that there will be activity in heaven. All such activity implies sequence and as long as there are sequential events, time remains relevant.

in the Flood, the Christ in the manger and then on the Cross, the conversion of Saul the Pharisee, the Dark Ages, Luther nailing his 95 Theses on the church door, William Carey getting off the boat in India, Billy Graham nervously preaching his first sermon and the antichrist being thrown into the lake of fire. It all sits under His eternal gaze. He is the great "I Am." Way back in the fourth century Augustine wrote:

> For not in our fashion does He look forward to what is future, nor what is present, nor back upon what is past; but in a manner quite different and far and profoundly remote from our way of thinking. For He does not pass from this to that by transition of thought, but beholds all things with absolute unchangeableness; so that of those things which emerge in time, the future indeed are not yet, and the present are now and the past no longer are; but all of these are by Him comprehended in his stable and eternal Presence.

The eternal realm in which God dwells knows no boundaries. He is infinite in every aspect of His character and Being. His presence, power, knowledge, love, grace and yes, even His wrath, are all endless. There are no limitations to any of them. A.W. Tozer describes man's errant perspective of the concept of infinity:

> We've got to eliminate all careless speech here. You and I talk about unlimited wealth, but there's no such thing; you can count it. We talk about boundless energy— which I don't feel I have at the moment—but there's no such thing; you can measure a man's energy. We say an artist takes infinite pains with his picture. But he doesn't take infinite pains; he just does the best he can and then throws up his hands and says, "It isn't right yet, but I'll have to let it go." That's what we call infinite pains.

But that is a misuse of the words "boundless," "unlimited" and "infinite." These words describe God—they don't describe anything *but* God.[5]

Whatever eternity is to man, it is something altogether different than it is for God. In some inexplicable way, God exists in an eternal realm outside of the time and eternity in which man lives. So we see that there are actually two different realms of existence which we call eternity.

Man's eternity will still be measured by increments of time. In that respect, it could be compared to space. Of course, we tend to think of space in terms of our daily lives: my driveway is about 1,000 feet long; it is an eight mile drive to the Pure Life Ministries campus from my home; it is about 2,000 miles to where I grew up in Sacramento, and so on.

However, to grasp the concept of infinitude we must get beyond the comfortable realm of life as we know it. Let's begin within our own solar system. It is approximately 284,000 miles to the moon and about 93 million miles to the sun. To measure anything beyond this, scientists had to come up with a bigger yardstick. It is called the light-year: the distance light can travel (at 186,000 miles *per second*) in one year. Or, to put it another way, one light-year is just under six trillion miles.

Now try to wrap your mind around this: just to travel across our galaxy, the Milky Way, would take 100,000 light-years! The *closest* galaxy beyond the Milky Way is Andromeda, 2 ½ million light-years away. But that is mere inches compared to Abell-2218, discovered by the Hubbell space telescope, which is 13 billion light-years away. The bottom line to all of this is that no matter how far out man might reach with his fancy telescopes, he cannot find the end to God's great universe.

In the same way, we cannot fathom the duration of eternity. Whatever it is, man is destined to continue living (either in everlasting bliss or damnation) forever and ever. John Wesley, who was always concerned about lost souls, offered this metaphor to illustrate the vastness of eternity:

> Suppose the ocean to be so enlarged, as to include all the space between the earth and the starry heavens. Suppose a drop of this water to be annihilated once in a thousand years; yet that whole space of duration, wherein this ocean would be annihilating, at the rate of one drop in a thousand years, would be infinitely less in proportion to eternity, than one drop of water to that whole ocean.
>
> Look then at those immortal spirits, whether they are in this or the other world. When they shall have lived thousands of thousands of years, yea, millions of millions of ages, their duration will be but just begun: They will be only upon the threshold of eternity![6]

The awareness of these great issues is actually considered a proof that a person has saving faith: "And it is after all only by faith," says the writer of Hebrews, "that our minds accept as fact that the whole scheme of time and space was created by God's command—that the world which we can see has come into being through principles which are invisible." (Hebrews 11:3 PHP)

GOD: UNCHANGING

The life of man is a long process of physical, emotional, mental and spiritual fluctuations and shifting changes. By the time he reaches the peak of his life, he has grown some twenty times his size at birth. He has developed even moreso mentally. He begins with zero knowledge—a blank slate—and by the end of his life his memory banks have accumulated millions of tidbits of information. He has also traveled a long road emotionally—all the way from the folly of youth to (hopefully) the wisdom of old age. Spiritually, he has either become increasingly more cynical and calloused or more godly and trusting.

This process of change is true with all of Nature. The fearful little cub tagging alongside his mother will one day become a powerful lion stalking its prey in the Serengeti. Mighty oak trees sprout forth as saplings, climb into the sky as monsters of the forest and end up decomposing on the rainforest floor. Given enough time, even the majestic Himalayas will dissolve into molehills. Everything created is continually undergoing the process of decay and change.

However, in His self-existent state, God does not change. The psalmist caught sight of this when he wrote:

> "O my God...Your years are throughout all generations. Of old You founded the earth, and the heavens are the work of Your hands. Even they will perish, but You endure; and all of them will wear out like a garment; like clothing You will change them and they will be changed. But You are the same, and Your years will not come to an end." (Psalm 102:24-27)

Creation ages and changes; the Creator does neither. Immutability is one aspect of God's self-existence. Moses wrote, "You are God without beginning or end."

Man becomes increasingly knowledgeable through life because he was utterly ignorant when he began life, but God is and has always been all-knowing. For Him to learn something would imply that there was a time when He lacked knowledge; that He was prone to making a mistake. His omniscient state of existence makes this impossible.

Furthermore, God's infinity precludes the possibility for Him to change. For instance, He is infinite in power; any lack of power would mean that He would be subject to gaining or losing power. His omnipotence is one further proof of His divinity.

This principle holds true regarding all of the Lord's attributes. His flawless character precludes any possibility of improvement. His perfect love means He cannot become more loving than He already is. His omnipresence rules out the possibility of there being some location He doesn't inhabit.

For God to change in any way would suggest that He could grow better or worse, He could become wiser or more foolish, He could be more honest or more deceiving and so on. The Lord will never be more or less than what He is at this very moment. He is perfect in all His ways and so shall He always be.

While the great kingdoms and societies of man arise and decline, God remains a great constant "through all the generations." This is a source of immense comfort to believers who live in a turbulent and fluctuating world. While He may somewhat alter the way He deals with different people groups during different ages, His character, His capacities and His overall purposes do not change. He is "the Father of lights, with whom there is no variation or shifting shadow." (James 1:17)

GOD: SOVEREIGN KING OF TIME AND HISTORY

Generations come and go. Mighty kingdoms emerge, only to grow complacent in their prosperity and are eventually overthrown by another. Ambitious kings occasionally rise up, conquer other nations, only to be vanquished themselves by another at a later date.

From His eternal vantage point, the Lord views the history of mankind in its entirety. He sees all the powerful rulers and great dynasties in an instant. The vast epochs of times gone by lay before Him.

Through it all God remains constant, His purposes immoveable. "God is the King of all the earth," said the psalmist. "God reigns over the nations, God sits on His holy throne." (Psalm 47:7-8) "It is He who changes the times and the epochs; He removes kings and establishes kings..." (Daniel 2:21) He is "the immortal and invisible King of the Ages." (I Timothy 1:17 WNT)

Paul told the Greek philosophers, "The God who made the world and all things in it...made from one man every nation of mankind to live on all the face of the earth, having determined their appointed times and the boundaries of their habitation..." (Acts 17:25-26) He later wrote, "For by Him all things were created, both in the heavens and on earth, visible and invisible, whether thrones or dominions or rulers or authorities—all things have been created through Him and for Him." (Colossians 1:16)

"I am God and there is no one like Me, declaring the end from the beginning, and from ancient times things which have not been done, saying, 'My purpose will be established, and I will accomplish all My good pleasure.'" (Isaiah 46:9-10)

"'I am the Alpha and the Omega,' says the Lord God, 'who is and who was and who is to come, the Almighty.'" (Revelation 1:8) In relation to man—the Lord is the beginning and ending and everything in between. This one sentence contains all that encompasses Time. He is the beginning of it; or, more accurately, He is the Creator of it. In the beginning, He initiated His grand program for mankind, and He will bring it to its conclusion. The very consummation of earth's ages will be wrapped up by the Lord Himself.

When one considers all that humankind's history has witnessed—the momentous events and all of the mundane acts of billions of souls, the great epochs of history and all of the fleeting moments of time, the great leaders and all of the common people, the Flood, the formation of Israel, the exile, the Birth and Death of Christ, the beginning of the Church, the Dark Ages, the closing scenes of Time—all of it has or will transpire under the ever watchful gaze of the Almighty.

Surely Moses was right when he said, "We glide along the tides of time as swiftly as a racing river and vanish as quickly as a dream. We are like grass that is green in the morning but mowed down and withered before the evening shadows fall." Or, to put it in the words of the psalmist, "O Lord, what is man, that You take knowledge of him? Or the son of man, that You think of him? Man is like a mere breath; His days are like a passing shadow." (Psalm 144:3-4)

Moses caught a glimpse of man's existence and all he could say was "man turns back to dust." There are no exceptions to the course of man. The angel of death comes for all: the small and great, the young and the old, the famous and unknown, the noble and reprobate; every man and woman returns to the dust. The Eternal watches it all unfold before His eyes. Man passes away but God continues.

"A little longer, and the godless
will be gone; look in his haunts, and
he is there no more! The land will be left
to the humble, to enjoy plenteous prosperity...
The Eternal...will advance you to possess
the land, and to see godless men exterminated."
    –David[1]

"God will wipe away every tear
from their eyes; and death shall be no more,
neither shall there be anguish (sorrow and mourning)
nor grief nor pain any more, for the old conditions
and the former order of things have passed away."
    –The Apostle John[2]

17

A RENOVATED PLANET

The hard times that befell England in the 1650's sent teeming masses of downtrodden people crowding into London.* The city was not prepared to handle this population explosion. By 1665, tenement buildings in slums like the West End had become scenes of filth and squalor. Garbage and human waste were simply dumped into the streets, providing a perfect breeding ground for rats. To make matters worse, it was an exceptionally hot summer that year; the city dwellers could do little to escape the blistering heat. It was then that rumors began circulating that there had been an outbreak of Plague in the city.

In their ignorance and superstition, people tried everything to contain the dread disease. One of the most common theories was that miasmas of poisonous air hung over the city, carrying the loathsome germs. Bon fires burned through the night in a futile attempt at cleansing the atmosphere. Another prevailing opinion was that dogs and cats were somehow responsible for

---

* If you haven't yet read the first appendix: "Books About Visits to Heaven," I strongly encourage you to do so before proceeding any further. I believe it will make the remainder of the book much more enjoyable.

the disease. Tens of thousands of animals were slaughtered, in the hopes of quelling the virus. Little did those unfortunate people know, but they were killing off the one predator of the real culprit: rats. It was a bacillus in the fleas which infested the rats that actually carried the Plague.

As the hot summer wore on, the bacteria flourished and the Plague ravaged. Victims were locked into their homes, their doors being marked with a large red cross. They expired within days, their final hours spent in agony and intense suffering. Every day dozens of bodies were hauled away and thrown into gruesome burning pits.

As the weather cooled that fall, the city was granted a temporary respite from the desolating disease. Unfortunately, as the temperature rose during the following summer, the Plague began to reemerge.

That September yet another calamity rocked the city. A fire broke out and quickly ravaged the thousands of wooden structures heaped up against each other throughout the metropolis. One by one entire city blocks were burnt to the ground. As is usually the case, the hardest hit neighborhoods were the slums—the very areas that were harboring the Plague.

People must have thought they were facing the very wrath of God. Actually, this new catastrophe was His mercy at work, for it was the very thing that eradicated the disease that had permeated and thrived within the rotten structures of the slums. The invisible destroyer was finally eliminated!

If we could but see the true condition of the human race, the overwhelming calamity that has befallen it would make the Plague of the 1660's seem like a minor nuisance. Ours is not a natural disease which kills a percentage of the population; it is a spiritual epidemic with a 100% mortality rate. Our pestilence does not typically bring about death within a week; it is a slow acting poison that brings with it a long and painful death. (James 1:15)

The discerning eye can see its devastating effects everywhere. Strife fills millions of homes. Children are ugly and malicious toward each other at school. The workforce is full of jealousy, competition and backbiting. The business sector is driven forward by merciless greed. The academic world fosters a superior, know-it-all form of pride. Ghettos are garrisons of conflict; their streets little more than war zones. Evil men rape defenseless children and then share pictures of their despicable crimes with each other on the Internet. The homosexual community continues to advance its agenda and lure millions of young people into its grip around the world. Selfishness and pride are the ruling passions of life everywhere one goes. The plague of sin continues to flourish, sending a million people into the cruel furnaces of hell every week. The truth is Planet Earth is one vast asylum of dying sinners. "The Lord saw that the wickedness of man was great on the earth, and that every intent of the thoughts of his heart was only evil continually." (Genesis 6:5; see also Matthew 24:37)

If there is any hope of reversing the Curse that has been unleashed on our planet, there is but one thing God can do: He must allow fire to burn out and eradicate every vestige of sin that has infested it. Little wonder Jesus exclaimed, "I have come to cast fire upon the earth; and how I wish it were already kindled!" (Luke 12:49) Peter predicted such a cataclysmic event: "But the day of the Lord will come like a thief, in which the heavens will pass away with a roar and the elements will be destroyed with intense heat, and the earth and its works will be burned up." (II Peter 3:10)

By and large, man has followed Satan in his insurrection with devastating consequences. We are quickly approaching the end of man's probationary period on earth. Satan and his foul legions have run riot within God's creation long enough. The Almighty is bringing everything under the feet of Christ. (Hebrews 2:8)

Our planet is about to undergo a conflagration that has never been seen. Those who love the ways of God welcome and long for the great day when every spiritual contaminate will be obliterated once and for all. (see I John 3:3)

In the same way the people of London "came through the fire" and were able to start life afresh with no remaining vestige of the Plague, so too will followers of Jesus Christ be handed a brand new world—completely free of every trace of sin—which will be a source of great joy for all eternity.

To digest the magnitude of such a proposition is no small matter. This world is all we have ever known. When we hear about a place like heaven, we have no point of reference. To help us grasp what lies "just over the hilltop," let us briefly consider how much the world in which we live is infected with sin and what it will be like to live without its malevolent touch.

THE END OF THE CURSE

It is difficult for us to comprehend how drastically life on this planet changed when God told Adam, "Cursed is the ground because of you..." (Genesis 3:17) From that moment on, something dreadful was set loose that turned earth into a Darwinian hell of survival of the fittest.

For instance, consider the animal kingdom. If you have ever viewed one of those heart-rending scenes on a nature show—where a predator chases and mauls to death some unfortunate victim—you are already aware of the savagery that dominates the animal kingdom. There will be animals in the New Earth, but its domain of death faces certain extinction:

> And the wolf will dwell with the lamb, and the leopard will lie down with the young goat, and the calf and the young lion and the fatling together; and a little boy will lead them. Also the cow and the bear will

graze, their young will lie down together, and the lion
will eat straw like the ox. The nursing child will play by
the hole of the cobra, and the weaned child will put his
hand on the viper's den. They will not hurt or destroy
in all My holy mountain, for the earth will be full of
the knowledge of the Lord as the waters cover the sea.
(Isaiah 11:6-9)†

The Curse not only affected animals, but it also seeped
into the entire microscopic world where germs, bacteria, fungi,
amoebas and insects flourish. Can you imagine never having to
deal with vermin, bugs or even germs? No need for pesticides
or insecticides there!

When you walk the golden streets of New Jerusalem, you
will not find one particle of dust, splotch of grime or sign
of filth anywhere. You will never encounter toxic chemical
fumes, noxious smog or the stench of sewage treatment plants.
Everything will be immaculately clean and in perfect order.

In fact, you will discover that the Second Law of
Thermodynamics will be permanently retired. That principle
states that everything within our universe is undergoing the
process of decay. Anything alive is in the process of dying;
anything with warmth is cooling; anything with energy is
being drained. There will be no such deterioration in heaven.
(Matthew 6:19-20)

Another aspect of our planet that we are accustomed to
facing is severe weather. Our planet has witnessed temperatures
from 130 degrees in the Sahara desert down to 130 degrees
below zero in Antarctica.

Not only must we endure harsh temperatures, but we also
must face nature's fury in the form of tornadoes, hurricanes,
earthquakes and tsunamis. Our world also produces occasional
droughts, leaving entire nations to face starvation.

---

† For a better comprehension of how this will affect the New Earth (after the Millennium) see
Randy Alcorn's book, *Heaven.*

How different will be the New Earth: a place of perfect weather all of the time! Perhaps our world will still enjoy the four seasons, but in some inexplicable way the weather will always be pleasant.

The Curse has also extended its malignant touch upon mankind. Once Adam rebelled against God's authority, he found the simplest tasks had become difficult. God told him, "you'll be working in pain all your life long." (Genesis 3:17 MSG) By contrast, our work in Paradise will be effortless. Many believers are gifted in certain forms of work; they will be allowed to further their careers there if that is what they desire. Whatever their heavenly tasks might be, they will certainly be thoroughly enjoyable and fulfilling.

I believe it is clear from Scripture that we will still have the desire for food and water, but we will eat and drink for the pure pleasure of it, not out of necessity. Likewise, sleep will be done from sheer contentedness. Those of us who deal with insomnia understand fully well how frustrating it is to get into bed exhausted from the stress and work of the day (and perhaps the sleeplessness of the night before), only to lay there wide awake! But sleep will always be a pleasant experience in heaven.

Actually, heaven will be a place of ineffable rest. Consider what the Word of God says about this:

- And so I would say to you who are suffering, God will give you rest along with us when the Lord Jesus appears suddenly from heaven…(II Thessalonians 1:7 LB)
- So then, there is still awaiting a full and complete Sabbath-rest reserved for the [*true*] people of God. (Hebrews 4:9 Amp)
- Yes, says the Spirit, let them rest from their sorrowful labours; for what they have done goes with them. (Revelation 14:13 WNT)

Surely one of the aspects of heaven will be rest from all our toil, as well as peace from all of our struggles. We will be like soldiers returning home after years of warfare, who can finally lay down their arms and spend the remainder of their lives living in tranquility.

THE END OF SIN

When you think about it, it is amazing that anyone can resist the temptation to sin during our time on earth. Consider the fact that we were born with a predisposition toward it. The world around us constantly lures us into its ungodly attractions. In addition, there are very powerful and relentless enemies operating in the unseen realm around us, at regular intervals dropping sinful suggestions into our minds. You and I live in this impossible situation everyday! If it wasn't for the grace of God there is simply no way we could survive the overwhelming temptations we regularly encounter.

But take a moment to contemplate what it will be like to have your heart utterly cleansed from every taint of sin and even the desire for it! In other words, once we cross into the hereafter, the inclination to transgress God's law—which is so natural to us now—will no longer be alive within us. As impossible as it is for a person to live a sin-free life now, that's how difficult it will be for a believer to sin in heaven. Not only will there be no outside source to allure us, but there will be no inward attraction toward it.

As Paul said, "But we are citizens of Heaven; our outlook goes beyond this world to the hopeful expectation of the Savior who...will re-make these wretched bodies of ours to resemble his own glorious body..." (Philippians 3:20-21 PHP) The apostle John added, "Yes, dear friends, we are already God's children, right now, and we can't even imagine what it is going to be like later on. But we do know this, that when he comes we will be like him, as a result of seeing him as he really is." (I John 3:2 LB)

Can you get your mind around those promises? What a glorious day it will be when the Lord extracts sin from our hearts—root and all!

We have become so accustomed to living under the tyranny of a sinful nature that it is hard for us to comprehend how much it affects the way we think and act. Consider one's tendency to look out for Number One; to exalt oneself at the expense of others; to emotionally protect oneself, no matter how it might hurt someone else to do it; to compete with others; to give over to feelings of envy, lust or resentment; to be impatient with or even lash out in anger at others. The list is endless. Our sinful flesh relentlessly compels us to pursue whatever it desires. The Christian's life on earth is one long battle with his own carnal desires. Not only must he deal with the direct and outward consequences of his sin, but then he must live afterwards with the resultant guilt and shame.

For the true believer, those days are coming to an end.

THE END OF PHYSICAL AND EMOTIONAL SUFFERING

If there is one companion every human being is well acquainted with throughout life it is pain. From the birthing process all the way to the throes of death it is intermittently encountered by all. In spite of our great familiarity with it, we still cringe when we feel its approach. It is amazing how something as simple as a headache or an upset stomach can ruin the most festive occasion. Suffering is a necessary part of earth life as it reminds us proud humans how frail we really are and compels us to look outside of ourselves for sustenance. And, of course, those of us who follow the Lord are benefitted by affliction because He uses it to develop godly character within us.

Pain and suffering can attach themselves to us in a thousand different ways. Think of the millions who are now languishing with cancer or some other deadly malady. Consider how many people hobble through life with the aftereffects of an injury sustained in younger years. How many people must live without sight or hearing? Think about all of the masses of people who suffer from malnourishment and its accompanying evils.

Physical affliction is terrible in itself, but sometimes emotional suffering can be even worse. Perhaps you know the pain of being jilted by a girlfriend (or boyfriend) or used by someone you trusted. Maybe you have been manipulated into doing something that was harmful to you or had someone you considered a friend turn on you. You might be one of the millions of people who go through life carrying the scars of childhood rejection or even physical or sexual abuse.

Disappointment is another form of suffering humans must face upon this planet. Think of the number of young people who begin life with bright hopes only to face one setback after another until they finally sink into a hopeless life of drudgery—far below their dreams. This is especially true for many young ministers who begin their careers with a sincere desire to win the world for Christ, but are beaten down by one blow after another until they give up inside and learn to go through the motions. Disappointment, discouragement or even depression lurk around the corner for everyone who lives in the realm dominated by the Evil One.

Then there is the family of fear, with all of its companions. Some people go through their entire lives dominated by nagging anxiety; a painful anticipation of something dreadful happening. Others suffer with a host of irrational phobias: fear of heights, germs, closed spaces and so on. Still others live with an inordinate trepidation of death.

One of the greatest sources of suffering is the loss of loved ones. Death stalks this planet like a roaring lion seeking whom it may devour. Every human lives with the certainty that his own days, as well as those of his loved ones, are numbered. It sometimes announces its impending attack months or even years ahead of time, as it systematically destroys a loved one's health. Then there are occasions when it strikes with no warning, leaving family and friends shocked and devastated.

Yes, our journey through this dark planet has a million forms of suffering lying in ambush along the way. Yet it is good for the believer to be reminded that the very best days we have lived during our stay on earth represent but a slight taste of what life will be like in that land of bliss.

Think of what it will be like to go through life knowing that you will never again face any form of suffering. How can we even comprehend such an existence? Life upon New Earth will be utterly free of pain, sickness and disease. We will be constantly protected from any kind of injury. Everyone we encounter will be kind, humble and full of love. No one will ever think a malicious or judgmental thought about us. There will be no competitive pride lurking in the hearts of those around us. We will encounter no Saul, no Ahithophel and no Absalom there. There will be no liars or false teachers in heaven. No one there will attempt to manipulate or take advantage of us.

We will look back upon the sufferings of earth life as a dark tunnel we had to traverse to arrive at our final home in heaven. But even the most painful memories will be softened in our minds by the Lord, who will wipe every tear from our eyes. (Revelation 7:17)

Upon our arrival in heaven, we will instantly realize how much fear we lived with on earth. All of the apprehensions we have carried with us through life will simply vanish. We will instinctively know that there is nothing to fear ever again. Even the angel of death will be banished from that glorious place. "O death, where then your victory? Where then your sting?" (I Corinthians 15:55 LB)

THE END OF THE USURPER

I suppose there might be occasions when it would be helpful to actually peer into the unseen realm surrounding us on earth, but I think I would prefer to just accept its existence by faith and let its features remain vague. If we could see some of the loathsome creatures that dog our every step, that scrutinize our every move, that constantly scheme to destroy us, we would probably be so traumatized that we would be ruined for life.

The Bible is fairly clear that we have a vicious enemy actively seeking to destroy us. We have devils who accuse us with condemning thoughts; allure us with sensuous enticements; plague us with irrational fears; bury us with discouragement, despair or depression; fan the flames of anger at every opportunity; attempt to distract our times of prayer, worship or Bible study; and plant evil, prideful, envious, lustful and even blasphemous thoughts into our minds.

Not only must we constantly face such mental struggles, but we must also live in a spiritual environment that is openly hostile to God's people. There is a powerful pressure to go along with the wicked mindset of our generation. The message to live for Self is unrelenting. Any attempt to stand outside of or, heaven forbid, *against* the rebel mindset of the world will be met with derision and cruelty. Everything in this fallen world has set itself against God's kingdom.

Living in a world dominated by the Evil One is difficult for everybody. Satan hates mankind because he knows we were created in the image of the God he despises. He and his minions lure people into their clutches, use them for their own purposes and then drag them into the eternal misery that they too must face.

Meanwhile, there are plenty of people who are given over—in one degree or another—to the devil's malicious ways. At the very least, every unbeliever helps to further the enemy's cause by simply living out the various "deeds of the flesh." But there are also dangerous and evil men who prowl our streets looking to victimize others. Worst of all are leaders in a position to bring suffering and destruction upon entire populations (e.g., Idi Amin, etc.).

We have all come to accept the fact that such evil people exist and do our utmost to avoid them. But can you imagine what it will be like to live in a world where injustice, war, crime and poverty are nonexistent? Think about the peace of mind you will enjoy knowing that your most vulnerable loved one can freely walk about on any street and at any hour without the slightest concern! Try to imagine living in a place where there is not one solitary person alive who is selfish, prideful, manipulative or malicious.

What will it be like to live under a government that is led by Jesus Christ and those who are most like Him? There will be no more backroom deals cut by unscrupulous politicians. There will be no more injustices perpetrated by those in positions of authority. There will be no more broken campaign promises or flaky leaders out for their own personal agendas.

The Savior—the very One who has done everything to secure our place in such a glorious world—will head up the worldwide government. His entire workforce, from top to bottom, will be made up of honest people sincerely serving their Leader and His people.

THE END OF THE VEIL

There is one final source of consternation believers must face on earth: the difficulty of following a Leader who dwells in an unseen realm.

On earth, one has to struggle against the natural tendency to drift away from God and into the world of sense. "All of us like sheep have gone astray," said the prophet, "each of us has turned to his own way." (Isaiah 53:6) This is the way of the sons of Adam.

Sometimes I think that I could handle any of the evils this world can dish out if only I consistently enjoyed the strong sense of God's presence in my life. Of course, I have had occasional mountaintop experiences when the glory of the Lord seemed to overtake my very being. Oh, what a tiny foretaste of life in the hereafter!

For the most part, however, we live out our lives in the swamps and bogs of a devil-infested world. We have a flesh nature that is like a thick layer of fat insulating us from feeling God's presence.

Let's face it, humans are fickle creatures. One day we feel passionate about the things of God, but the very next day we go into a funk over the most trivial incident. One moment we feel God's love flowing out toward those we encounter and the next we want to avoid everyone. Every aspect of the Christian life seems to constantly fluctuate for the best of us.

Then there are those times when the Lord purposely withdraws the sense of His presence. I can't think of anything more devastating for a sincere believer than to experience the deadness of soul when God pulls away.

During our stay on earth, we must walk by faith and not by sight. (II Corinthians 5:7) "For now we see in a mirror dimly, but then face to face..." (I Corinthians 13:12) Truly, there is a veil over the eyes of our heart.

For your entire Christian life, your relationship with the Lord has been lived through the eyes of faith. Can you imagine what it will be like to see Him face to face? Think of what your spiritual life will be like when everywhere you go you encounter people who love Him; where everything in your environment encourages your devotion to Him; where spiritual vitality fills the very air you breathe.

Have you ever been in a worship service where God's presence was so strong that you could actually feel it? I believe that heaven will be just like that, only much more intense than anything we have experienced upon earth. The sweet aroma of God will pervade every region of heaven.

Yes, we have been forced to cohabitate with many forms of evil on this planet, but one day the fire of God will burn out every taint of sin and leave us a beautiful place to call home.

*"For the Kingdom of God is not
a matter of what we eat or drink,
but of living a life of goodness and peace
and joy in the Holy Spirit."*
–the Apostle Paul[1]

*"So the ransomed of the Lord
will return and come with joyful shouting
to Zion, and everlasting joy will be on their heads.
They will obtain gladness and joy, and
sorrow and sighing will flee away."*
–Isaiah[2]

18

INTO THE WORLD OF LOVE

S amuel Morrison spent 25 years on the African continent as a missionary. In that span of time he had witnessed the death of many of his beloved colleagues; suffered terrible deprivation; had been violently ill many times; and had given his life to people who often responded with indifference or even treachery.

At long last he boarded the ocean liner which would return him to America. His health was broken and he looked forward to spending his remaining years in semi-retirement. As the ship began its approach into New York harbor, he noticed a large crowd of well-wishers waiting at the dock. There were people who knew of his homecoming, but he never expected a reception like this! His excitement grew with anticipation. As the ship drew closer, he was finally able to make out one of the banners.

His heart sank.

They weren't there to welcome him at all. Teddy Roosevelt was on the ship, returning from a hunting safari and the celebration was for his return. For a brief moment, he indulged in a bout of self-pity. "Lord," he whimpered, "couldn't I have had just one welcoming home party?"

The Lord immediately spoke to his heart, "Who said you're home?" The reality that America was only another stopover on his journey toward his true home burst into his heart. He would have a homecoming party, but it would be up yonder, not in America.

So it will be with every weary soldier going home after the long years of warfare. They won't return to a ticker tape parade in New York City, the joy of which is sure to diminish within days. No, theirs will be a hero's welcome that will be burned into their memory forever. "Things no eye has seen, no ear has heard, no human heart conceived, the welcome God has prepared for those who love him." (I Corinthians 2:9 Knox) Charles Spurgeon offers the following picture of that great moment:

> The Christian's battlefield is here, but the triumphal procession is above. This is the land of the garment rolled in blood and of the dust of the fight: that is the land of the white robe and of the shout of conquest. O, what a thrill of joy shall be felt by all the blessed when their conquests shall be complete in heaven; when Satan shall be dragged captive at the chariot wheels of Christ; when the great shout of universal victory shall rise from the hearts of all the redeemed! What a moment of pleasure shall that be![3]

The certainty of our glorious welcome above is not built upon our efforts—no matter how noble they might have been; it is grounded upon the sure foundation of God's love. Consider how much time, effort and resources the Lord has invested into the soul of one of His children. It began with years of heart preparation and conviction of sin before the person finally surrendered his heart and will to God. A great shout of joy sounded forth in heaven when that happened. (Luke 15:7) For a number of years afterward the Lord built a solid foundation under the person as he grew in his newfound faith. The Holy Spirit continued working inside him and through him for the rest of his life. All of this effort was expended because of God's great love for him. Finally, the beloved saint reached the final "dot on his line." It was time for his passing over. Can you see how the Lord would be excited about this day? Surely this is what the psalmist meant when he wrote, "Precious in the sight of the Lord is the death of His godly ones." (Psalm 116:15)

Of course, what actually occurs for a person who passes into the hereafter is obscure to us mortals. Still, there have been enough fragments of evidence to give us an idea about what to expect. For instance, when the Lord told the story about the death of Lazarus the beggar, He said that he "was carried away by the angels to Abraham's bosom." (Luke 16:22)

In his work as a minister over the years, Charles Finney witnessed the death of a number of Christians. The following are his reflections on the death experience:

> If it be true that angels convey saints to heaven, as we are taught in God's word, then it is not irrational to suppose that what many saints say in their dying hours of the things they see, is strictly true. Gathering darkness clouds the senses, and the mind becomes greatly spiritual, as their looks plainly show. Those looks—the eye, the countenance, the melting whisper, these tell the story better than any words can do it; indeed, no words can describe those *looks*—no language can paint what you can stand by and see and hear—a peace so deep and so divine; this shows that the soul is *almost* in heaven. In all ages it has been common for some dying saints to hear music which they supposed to be of heaven, and to see angels near and around them. With eyes that see what others cannot see, they recognize their attending angels as already come.

"Don't *you* hear that music?" say they. "Don't you see those shining ones? they come, they come!"[4]

Apparently not everyone is met by angels when they die. During World War II an unsaved recruit named George Ritchie died of pneumonia in an army hospital.* He tells the story of his initial experience upon discovering that he was separated from his lifeless body lying on a bed.

There, right there, was my own shape and substance, yet as distant from me as though we inhabited separate planets. Was this what death was? This separation of one part of a person from the rest of him?

I wasn't sure when the light in the room began to change; suddenly I was aware that it was brighter, a lot brighter, than it had been. I whirled to look at the nightlight on the bedside table. Surely a single 15-watt bulb couldn't turn out that much light?

I stared in astonishment as the brightness increased, coming from nowhere, seeming to shine everywhere at once. All the light bulbs in the ward couldn't give off that much light. All the bulbs in the world couldn't! It was impossibly bright: it was like a million welders' lamps all blazing at once. And right in the middle of my amazement came a prosaic thought probably born of some biology lecture back at the university: "I'm glad I don't have physical eyes at this moment," I thought. "This light would destroy the retina in a tenth of a second."

No, I corrected myself, not the light.

He.

He would be too bright to look at. For now I saw that it was not light but a Man who had entered the

---

* George Ritchie had a powerful experience with the Lord. He was allowed a second chance at life, surrendered his heart to God and later became a renowned psychiatrist.

room, or rather, a Man made out of light, though this seemed no more possible to my mind than the incredible intensity of the brightness that made up His form.

The instant I perceived Him, a command formed itself in my mind. "Stand up!" The words came from inside me, yet they had an authority my mere thoughts had never had. I got to my feet, and as I did came the stupendous certainty: "You are in the presence of *the* Son of God."[5]

Rebecca Springer had a similar experience. She had been a dedicated believer for many years when she died after weeks of illness. It wasn't the Lord or an angel who met her, but her long-since deceased brother-in-law. She quickly became overwhelmed with gratitude as she entered that land of bliss.

> "Oh, Frank,..." such an overpowering sense of God's goodness and my own unworthiness swept over me that I dropped my face into my hands, and burst into uncontrollable and very human weeping.
>
> "Ah!" said my brother, in a tone of self-reproach, "I am inconsiderate." And lifting me gently to my feet, he said, "Come, I want to show you the river."...
>
> I drew back timidly, saying, "I fear it is cold."
>
> "Not in the least," he said, with a reassuring smile. "Come."
>
> "Just as I am?" I said, glancing down at my lovely robe, which, to my great joy, I found was similar to those of the dwellers in that happy place.
>
> "Just as you are," with another reassuring smile.
>
> Thus encouraged, I, too, stepped into the 'gently flowing river,' and to my great surprise found the water, in both temperature and density, almost identical with

the air. Deeper and deeper grew the stream as we passed on, until I felt the soft, sweet ripples playing about my throat. As I stopped, my brother said, "A little farther still."

"It will go over my head," I expostulated.

"Well, and what then?"

"I cannot breathe under the water—I will suffocate."

An amused twinkle came into his eyes, though he said soberly enough, "We do not do those things here."

I realized the absurdity of my position, and with a happy laugh said, "All right; come on," and plunged headlong into the bright water, which soon bubbled and rippled several feet above my head. To my surprise and delight, I found I could not only breathe, but laugh and talk, see and hear, as naturally under the water as above it...

"What marvelous water!... Frank, what has that water done for me?" I said. "I feel as though I could fly."

He looked at me with earnest, tender eyes, as he answered gently, "It has washed away the last of the earth-life, and fitted you for the new life upon which you have entered."[6]

Betty Maltz is another believer who experienced death and was subsequently allowed to return to earth life. In 1959, at the age of 27, she died from the complications of a burst appendix. The following incident describes Betty's approach to the gates of heaven.

The transition was serene and peaceful. I was walking up a beautiful green hill...

"Can this be death?" I wondered. If so I certainly

had nothing to fear. There was no darkness, no uncertainty, only a change in location and a total sense of well-being.

All around me was a magnificent deep blue sky, unobscured by clouds. Looking about, I realized that there was no road or path. Yet I seemed to know where to go.

Then I realized I was not walking alone. To the left, and a little behind me, strode a tall, masculine-looking figure in a robe. I wondered if he were an angel...

The angel stepped forward and put the palm of his hand upon a gate which I had not noticed before. About twelve feet high, the gate was a solid sheet of pearl, with no handles and some lovely scroll work at the top of its Gothic structure. The pearl was translucent so that I could almost, but not quite, see inside. The atmosphere inside was somehow filtered through. My feeling was of ecstatic joy and anticipation at the thought of going inside.

When the angel stepped forward, pressing his palm on the gate, an opening appeared in the center of the pearl panel and it slowly widened and deepened as though the translucent material was dissolving. Inside I saw what appeared to be a street of golden color with an overlay of glass or water. The yellow light that appeared was dazzling. There is no way to describe it. I saw no figure, yet I was conscious of a Person. Suddenly I knew that the light was Jesus, the Person was Jesus.

I did not have to move. The light was all about me. There seemed to be some heat in it as if I were standing in sunlight; my body began to glow. Every part of me was absorbing the light. I felt bathed by the rays of a powerful, penetrating, loving energy.[7]

A WORLD OF JOY

Every account I have read of people entering heaven has related the same sense of well-being. What is it about that place that creates such an atmosphere? Obviously heaven is the home of the God of love. His presence establishes the environment there.

David seemed to have a premonition of the wonderful atmosphere of heaven when he wrote, "Thou wilt reveal the path of life, to the full joy of thy presence, to the bliss of being close to thee forever." (Psalm 16:11 Mof) Yes, a world of "full joy"—the joy of the Lord! The Pulpit Commentary brings out the source of this joy and how it is possible to catch glimpses of it even on earth:

GOD HAS JOY. He is not indifferent, nor is he morose; we are to think of him as the "blessed" God, i.e., as essentially happy. The brightness and beauty of the world are reflections from the blessedness of God. Because he is glad, nature is glad, flowers bloom, birds sing, young creatures bound with delight. Nothing is more sad in perversions of religion than the representations of God as a gloomy tyrant. Less terrible, but scarcely less false, are those monkish ideas which deny the tyranny but cherish the gloom of a somber divinity more suited to chill, dark cloisters than to that glorious temple of nature in which the eternal presence dwells and manifests himself symbolically. These fragrant meadows, broad rolling seas of moorland heather, rich green forest cities of busy insect life, flashing ocean waves, and the pure blue sky above, and all that is sweet and lovely in creation, spell one symphony of gladness, because the mighty Spirit that haunts them is himself overflowing with joy. Our God is a *Sun*. And if divinity is sunny, so should religion be. The happy God will rejoice in the happiness of his children. Innocent mirth, though forbidden by Puritan sourness, can be no offence to such a God. The typical citizens of his kingdom are little children; and what is so joyous as childhood?[8]

If God's joyous nature can still be glimpsed on this cursed planet, what will it be like when it abounds unabated? And what will it be like when He can freely dispense gifts to His children? Of course He is forced to restrain His natural generosity during our earth stay, but then, He will be able to give full sway to His magnanimous heart!

David wrote, "How great is the goodness you have stored up for those who fear you. You lavish it on those who come to you for protection, blessing them before the watching world." (Psalm 31:19 NLT) The Lord possesses an inexhaustible supply of goodness. We can no more exhaust His storehouse of blessing than we could drink the Mississippi River dry. His goodness is just as infinite as eternity itself.

"O taste and see that the Lord is good," (Psalm 34:8) exclaims the psalmist. And perhaps on earth all we can hope for is a taste, but what will it be like to be immersed in His goodness? "Surely goodness and lovingkindness will follow me all the days of my life," (Psalm 23:6) he says, but what will happen when they finally catch up and absolutely overwhelm us? "No good thing does He withhold from those who walk uprightly," (Psalm 84:11) but what will it be like when He finally has the liberty to present us with all the good things He has long desired to give us? Yes, He "satisfies [our] years with good things," (Psalm 103:5) but what will it be like after ten thousand such years?

A.W. Tozer wrote, "The true Christian may safely look forward to a future state that is as happy as perfect love wills it to be. Since love cannot desire for its object anything less than the fullest possible measure of enjoyment for the longest possible time, it is virtually beyond our power to conceive of a future as consistently delightful as that which Christ is preparing for us. And who is to say what is possible with God?"[9]

Of course, God's joyful, giving Spirit is the natural outflow of His great heart of love. "God is love," the apostle tells us. (I John 5:8) God's loving presence will be the very atmosphere of heaven.

Yes, we will feel His lovingkindness all of the time, but it goes even beyond that. His love will create an environment where the natural interaction between the citizens of heaven will be a deep sense of devotion to each other. Consider what it will be like when the principles outlined in the "Love Chapter" are the corporate mindset of every person abiding in the community:

> This love of which I speak is slow to lose patience— it looks for a way of being constructive. It is not possessive: it is neither anxious to impress nor does it cherish inflated ideas of its own importance. Love has good manners and does not pursue selfish advantage. It is not irritable or touchy. It does not hold grudges and will hardly even notice when others do it wrong. On the contrary, it is glad with all good men when truth prevails. Love knows no limit to its endurance, no end to its trust, no fading of its hope; it can outlast anything. It is, in fact, the one thing that still stands when all else has fallen. (I Corinthians 13:4-8a LB & PHP)[†]

Can you see what a beautiful atmosphere this will create among God's people? It should be noted that the law of sowing and reaping operates as much (or more) within a community as it does in an individual's life.

---

† I was hard-pressed to choose between the Philips translation and the Living Bible, so I used a combination of statements from both.

Unfortunately, our experience with this principle on a corporate level has been mostly negative. The prison world is an extreme example of the negative aspect of this law in operation. Penitentiary life is a world unto itself which is governed by a convoluted value system. It honors its most ruthless members, their every brutal deed further embedding this cruel mindset amongst its inhabitants.

As hellish as that can be, can you imagine what it would be like to live in a culture where the exact opposite mentality is entrenched? The happy citizens there will not have to deal with self-centeredness or pride—their own or anyone else's. Showing kindness will not be the exception, or even the occasional; it will be the everyday norm. And, just like the opposite holds true in a place like prison, every merciful deed will only deepen a corporate mindset of love. As Isaiah said, "The righteous will be happy, and things will go well for them. They will get to enjoy what they have worked for." (Isaiah 3:10 GNB)

One of the most blessed aspects of life in heaven surely must be the prevailing mindset of kindness amongst God's people. In Luke 6:38, Jesus offered the sowing-and-reaping principle with a little more detail. Consider the truth of this verse in terms of how it must be in effect within heaven's community. The following paraphrases bring it out more fully:

- Give to others, and God will give to you. Indeed, you will receive a full measure, a generous helping, poured into your hands—all that you can hold. The measure you use for others is the one that God will use for you. (GNB)
- Give away your life; you'll find life given back, but not merely given back—given back with bonus and blessing. Giving, not getting, is the way. Generosity begets generosity. (MSG)

- For if you give, you will get! Your gift will return to you in full and overflowing measure, pressed down, shaken together to make room for more, and running over. Whatever measure you use to give—large or small—will be used to measure what is given back to you. (LB)

Can you imagine what it will be like to live in such a happy world? What will it be like for the "group think" of an entire population to be dominated by the sweet Holy Spirit? Everything around you will constantly encourage love and godliness.

Yes, heaven will surely be a world of joy, but it will also be a world of happy activity!

*"And I, John, saw the Holy City,
the new Jerusalem, coming down from God
out of heaven. It was a glorious sight, beautiful
as a bride at her wedding."*
—The Apostle John[1]

*"I, with shriveled, bent fingers,
atrophied muscles, gnarled knees, and
no feeling from the shoulders down,
will one day have a new body,
light, bright, and clothed in righteousness—
powerful and dazzling. Can you
imagine the hope this gives someone
spinal-cord injured like me?"*
—Joni Eareckson Tada[2]

DAILY LIFE IN NEW JERUSALEM

As our Creator, God loves to design and produce things that are going to be a blessing to the ones He loves. One can only imagine how tremendous the plans are of the city He has drafted for us! Abraham, the father of our faith, pressed through many hard years of nomadic life because he believed this: "For he was looking for the city which has foundations, whose architect and builder is God." (Hebrews 11:10)

During the Last Supper, Jesus said, "In My Father's house are many dwelling places; if it were not so, I would have told you; for I go to prepare a place for you. If I go and prepare a place for you, I will come again and receive you to Myself, that where I am, there you may be also." (John 14:2-3) We are destined to be citizens of a marvelous, bustling, joyous metropolis which God has prepared for us.

But what do we know about this celestial city? "We understand cities. Cities have buildings, culture, art, music, athletics, goods and services, events of all kinds. And, of course, cities have people engaged in activities, gatherings, conversations, and work."[3]

In the center of New Jerusalem will be the Throne of God

and an enormous park surrounding it. The apostle John was offered a glimpse of this. "And he pointed out to me a river of pure Water of Life, clear as crystal, flowing from the throne of God and the Lamb, coursing down the center of the main street. On each side of the river grew Trees of Life, bearing twelve crops of fruit, with a fresh crop each month; the leaves were used for medicine to heal the nations." (Revelation 22:1-2 LB)

Apparently this lovely park was one of the first sections of heaven visited by the Chinese children H.A. Baker wrote about. They called it Paradise:

> One of the young men was in Paradise almost as soon as he entered the heavenly city. There he was met by the two Adullam boys who had died in Hokow. These boys, taking him through Paradise and the other parts of the Holy City, soon came to a great, lawn-like, grassy, open plot surrounded by magnificent trees.
>
> The whole scene was so entrancing that the young man said to his two glorified friends, "This is good enough for me. There can't be anything more beautiful. I'll stay right here.
>
> The boys who had preceded him to heaven said, "No, don't wait here, for there are much greater marvels."
>
> Going on a little farther they came to still more wonderful trees, some of them bearing fruit. The whole park-like surroundings and the grassy lawn beneath the trees were enticing beyond any earthly understanding.
>
> The young man said, "I must stay here, I cannot go on and leave this great beauty. I am so happy."
>
> "Come on," said the others, "there are many things in heaven exceeding this."
>
> "You go," he replied, "but I shall remain right here for awhile."
>
> The others left him on the grass under the trees

with the great, open, velvet-like grassy space before him. Floods of joy and happiness he had never known on earth flooded his whole being. He was in the land of joy, "joy unspeakable and full of glory," "the land that is fairer than day."[4]

Rebecca Springer also was allowed to visit the holy city one day when her brother-in-law offered to escort her there. She excitedly joined him on the short trek to the city.

Passing up a slight acclivity, we found ourselves in a broad street that led into the heart of the city. The streets I found were all very broad and smooth, and paved with marble and precious stones of every kind. Though they were thronged with people intent on various duties, not an atom of debris, or even dust, was visible anywhere. There seemed to be vast business houses of many kinds, though I saw nothing resembling our large mercantile establishments.

There were many colleges and schools; many book and music-stores and publishing houses; several large manufactories, where, I learned, were spun the fine silken threads of manifold colors which were so extensively used in the weaving of the draperies I have already mentioned. There were art rooms, picture galleries and libraries, and many lecture halls and vast auditoriums. But I saw no churches of any kind. At first this somewhat confused me, until I remembered that there are no creeds in heaven, but that all worship together in harmony and love – the children of one and the same loving Father...

We found no dwelling-houses anywhere in the midst of the city, until we came to the suburbs. Here they stood in great magnificence and splendor. But one pleasing fact was that every home had its large door-yard, full of trees and flowers and pleasant walks; indeed, it was everywhere, outside of the business center of the town, like one vast park dotted with lovely houses. There was much that charmed, much that surprised me in this great city, of which I may not fully speak, but which I never can forget.

We found in one place a very large park, with walks and drives and fountains and miniature lakes and shaded seats, but not dwellings or buildings of any kind, except an immense circular open temple capable of seating many hundred; and where, my brother told me, a seraph choir assembled at a certain hour daily and rendered the oratories written by the great musical composers of earth and heaven. It had just departed, and the crowd who had enjoyed its divine music yet lingered as though loath to leave a spot so hallowed.[5]

While New Jerusalem will certainly be laden with such restful locales, it would be wrong to think of it as a place where saints do nothing but lay around strumming harps! Actually, a large part of our time will be taken up with joyful, meaningful work:

> On the New Earth, God will give us renewed minds and marvelously constructed bodies. We'll be whole people, full of energy and vision…
>
> In Heaven, we'll reign with Christ, exercise leadership and authority, and make important decisions. This implies we'll be given specific responsibilities by our leaders and we'll delegate specific responsibilities to those under our leadership (Luke 19:17-19). Our best work days on the present Earth—those days when everything turns out better than we planned, when we get everything done on time, and when everyone on the team pulls together and enjoys each other—are just

a small foretaste of the joy our work will bring us on the New Earth…[6]

SOCIAL ACTIVITIES IN THE HEREAFTER

Life in America has greatly changed over the past fifty years. When I grew up as a child, everyone in the neighborhood knew each other. Neighbors weren't necessarily good friends, but there was enough regular interaction that they knew what to expect from each other. It was very common for people to while away the evening hours chatting with neighbors on their front porch.

That is a bygone era for most people. The increased mobility of our culture has encouraged folks to spend their leisure time with people of similar interests and viewpoints—even if they live miles away.

When people do stay home, television programming or the Internet keep them locked inside. Even kids have been affected by this mindset. They are more likely to be found in front of a computer or intense video game than out in the sandlot playing ball or fixing up a dollhouse with a girlfriend.

All of this has greatly changed the social landscape of the United States. As people have increasingly detached from each other, a growing sense of mistrust has become established in our culture.[*] People tend to be much more wary about others than they used to be.

American believers will be in for a very pleasant surprise when they arrive in heaven. All distrust for other people will quickly die out because it will be so obvious that no one there would ever think of trying to take advantage of another. As we saw in the last chapter, God's goodness will establish the environment of all social interaction.

---

* One of the aspects of hell in C.S. Lewis's brilliant book *The Great Divorce* was that over the ages of eternity people would grow further and further away from each other until they were lost in a vast space millions of miles away from their nearest neighbor.

I do believe we will have forms of healthy entertainment. They will have their time and place, but no one in heaven will become obsessed with them (e.g., teenagers in a carnal frenzy over a video game). In some ways, I suspect that life will be similar to the pleasant days of the '50s and '60s when neighbors were more likely to enjoy spending time together.

Also, everyone there will have the same basic viewpoints and attitudes about life. People will still see things from their own perspectives, but they won't feel a prideful need to push their opinions on others. Imagine what a blessing it will be to fellowship with other Christians without any concern about doctrinal differences or judgmental attitudes. Whatever else might be the case, heaven will be a place of great harmony and unity.

There will be so many different things people will be able to do together. We will have picnics, cookouts, softball games, swimming parties, mountain hikes, bicycle rides and an endless assortment of other activities that we cannot even imagine. Someone even suggests the possibility of travel to one of the billions of planets that make up the universe. Whatever we do, we are sure to have good, wholesome fun with each other. As Jesus said, "What happiness there is for you who weep, for the time will come when you shall laugh with joy!" (Luke 6:21 LB) Randy Alcorn brings out this cheerful aspect of heaven life:

> "If you're not allowed to laugh in heaven, I don't want to go there." It wasn't Mark Twain who said that. It was Martin Luther…
>
> When laughter is prompted by what's appropriate, God always takes pleasure in it. I think Christ will laugh with us, and his wit and fun-loving nature will be our greatest source of endless laughter…
>
> Take any group of rejoicing people, and what do you hear? Laughter. There may be hugging, backslapping, playful wrestling, singing, and storytelling. But always there is laughter. It is God's gift to humanity, a gift

that will be raised to new levels after our bodily resurrection...

God won't only wipe away all our tears, he'll fill our hearts with joy and our mouths with laughter.[7]

No matter who we socialize with, it is sure to be one positive experience after another. Of course, we will have many new friends. Imagine spending hours swapping anecdotes with an Old Testament saint. Think about talking to one of the Christians who were healed by Jesus and became a member of the Early Church. What would it be like to fellowship with a brother who faced Nero's persecution or a Russian sister who suffered under the tyranny of communism? What a joy it would be to hear the stories of those who were saved from jungle tribes or Muslim nations.

Undoubtedly there will also be opportunities to spend time with renowned saints such as Samuel, David, Moses, Daniel, Paul, Martin Luther, William Carey or Amy Carmichael. They are all there! None of them will carry an air of superiority either. Jesus alluded to this when He said, "I say to you that many will come from east and west, and recline at the table with Abraham, Isaac and Jacob in the kingdom of heaven." (Matthew 8:11) Who are coming from the east and west? You and me!

Most of all, heaven will be a place of wonderful reunions with loved ones. Rebecca Springer describes meeting her family there soon after her arrival. It happened one day when her brother-in-law asked her who she most wanted to see:

"My father and mother," I answered quickly.

He smiled so significantly that I hastily turned, and there, advancing up the long room to meet me, I saw my dear father and mother, and with them my youngest sister. With a cry of joy, I flew into my father's outstretched arms, and heard, with a thrill of joy, his dear, familiar "My precious little daughter!"

"At last! At last!" I cried, clinging to him. "At last I have you again!"

"At last!" he echoed, with a deep-drawn breath of joy. Then he resigned me to my dear mother, and we were soon clasped in each other's embrace.

"My precious mother!" "My dear, dear child!" we cried simultaneously; and my sister enfolding us both in her arms, exclaimed with a happy laugh, "I cannot wait! I will not be left outside!" and disengaging one arm, I threw it about her into the happy circle of our united love.[8]

THE REAL "CITY OF ANGELS"

Yes, heaven will be a place of wonderful, happy people. But humans aren't the only inhabitants of that joyful land. Angels live there as well.

Scripture makes it clear that angels play a huge role in God's economy. They were present when the Lord created earth and were so excited by His creative exploits that "they shouted for joy." (Job 38:7) On earth they have operated as God's messengers (Matthew 1:20) and also as the deliverers of divine judgment (II Samuel 24:16; II Kings 19:35; Ezekiel 9; etc.). They watch over God's elect (Psalm 91:11) and undertake their cause when necessary. (Hebrews 1:14; Acts 5:19) They will accompany Jesus Christ in His return to earth (Matthew 25:31) and will also be the agents who separate the wicked from the godly. (Matthew 13:49) In general, angels function as the Lord's agents in accomplishing His good will.[†]

When the little Chinese orphans visited heaven, they were especially enthralled with the many angels they encountered:

---

† The apostle Paul said that Christians will judge the angels. (I Corinthians 6:3) That little statement tells us that angels are not "automons." In other words, they have the capacity to make decisions for themselves. If their efforts during the course of this world's history are to be judged, then it stands to reason that some angels will fulfill their duties with more earnestness than others.

Through the gates into the city! Out of earth into heaven! Out of the mortal into the immortal! Out of death into life! All the old life behind and below! All the new life ahead and above! Inside the gates! Angels, angels everywhere. Angels talking, angels singing, angels rejoicing, angels playing harps and blowing trumpets, angels dancing and praising the King. Such a scene no mortal ever saw; such a flood of inner joy as no one ever knew flooded the whole being...

Frequently an angel came walking by, playing a harp and singing. The angel smiled, offered him the harp. "I cannot play," he said. The angel passed by. Soon other angels came, smiling to him as they played and sang.

The angels were dressed in seamless garments of white; their faces were perfect; one was not more beautiful than another. "When they smiled—Oh, I can't describe that," the boy said later, "there is no way on earth to describe an angel's smile."[9]

Billy Graham was so taken up with the subject of angels that he devoted an entire book to the study of them. One of the great roles he discovered that they play is worship:

Angels possess the ultimate capacity to offer praise, and their music from time immemorial has been the primary vehicle of praise to our all-glorious God. Music is the universal language. It is likely that John saw a massive heavenly choir (Revelation 5:11, 12) of many millions who expressed their praise of the heavenly Lamb through magnificent music.

While it is partly speculative, I believe that angels have the capacity to employ heavenly celestial music. Many dying believers have testified that they have heard the music of heaven...

We can look for that future day when angels will have finished their earthly ministry. Then they will gather with all the redeemed before the throne of God in heaven. There they will offer their praise and sing their songs...they sing; my, how they sing![10]

Annie Schisler often caught glimpses of various ranks of angelic beings in the visions she received. Some were very powerful beings who executed God's solemn judgments. Others performed more mundane duties. None of her experiences with them could have prepared her for the whimsical moment the Lord allowed her to enjoy at the hands of a group of angels:

I found myself in a vast field. The field looked like it was made of some beautiful cloth made out of cottony clouds of light that both lived and moved and irradiated light. How strange and how far removed from any substance found in this earth. It was a field that looked so glorious...There were other angels there with Jesus that did not enter into this play or game or whatever it was. Jesus watched us like a loving Father watches His children play but He did not participate...

Suddenly I was with a group of these angels in this vast field and they began to play with me. They carried me in their arms and with great tenderness and great swiftness of flight they rushed back and forth over this great field passing me from one to another. I felt like I was floating. All laughed and with much pleasure and joy. For a long while at great speeds they covered that huge field of strange material from side to side, back and forth, passing me from one to another always with great tenderness. I found myself laughing with joy with them.[11]

WORSHIP SERVICES

Of course, when we talk about the great delight of fellowshipping with loved ones and enjoying the company of angels, we will certainly remember He who made all of this possible. Every morning we wake up in this land of bliss, we will surely be overcome with gratitude to the One who paid for it all with His blood.

Can you imagine the enormous amount of gratitude that will energize the worship services in heaven? We will never tire of expressing our love and praise to Him. Every activity in heaven will have a sense of spirituality that accompanies it, but there will also be those occasions when our entire attention is focused on God alone. Rebecca Springer describes one such experience when her brother-in-law took her to an enormous auditorium to hear Martin Luther speak. It is a fitting story with which to end this chapter.

His discourse would of itself fill a volume, and could not be given even in outline, in this brief sketch. He held us enthralled by the power of his will and his eloquence. When at length he retired, John Wesley took his place, and the saintly beauty of his face, intensified by the heavenly light upon it, was wonderful. His theme was "God's love;" and if in the earth-life he dwelt upon it with power, he now swept our souls with the fire of his exaltation, until we were as wax in his hands. He showed what that love had done for us, and how an eternity of thanksgiving and praise could never repay it.

Silence, save for the faint, sweet melody of the unseen choir, rested upon the vast audience for some time after he left. All seemed lost in contemplation of the theme so tenderly dwelt upon. Then the heavy curtains back of the platform parted, and a tall form, about whom all the glory of heaven seemed to center, emerged from their folds and advanced toward the middle of the platform. Instantly the vast concourse of souls arose to their feet, and burst forth as...a grand chorus of voices, [with] such unity, such harmony, such volume, [as] was never heard on earth. It rose, it swelled, it seemed to fill not only the great auditorium, but heaven itself. And still, above it all, we heard the voices of the angel choir, no longer breathing the soft, sweet melody, but bursting forth into paeans of triumphant praise. A flood of glory seemed to fill the place, and looking upward we beheld the great dome ablaze with golden light...

As I looked upon the glorious form before us, clothed in all the majesty of the Godhead, my heart tremblingly asked: "Can this indeed be the Christ-man whom Pilate condemned to die an ignominious death upon the cross?" I could not accept it. It seemed impossible that any man, however vile, could be blind to the divinity so plainly revealed in him.

Then the Savior began to speak, and the sweetness of his voice was far beyond the melody of the heavenly choir. And his gracious words! Would that I could, would that I dared, transcribe them as they fell from his lips. Earth has no language by which to convey their lofty meaning. He first touched lightly upon the earth-life, and showed so wonderfully the link of light uniting the two lives—the past with the present. Then he unfolded to us some of the earlier mysteries of the blessed life, and pointed out the joyous duties just before us.

When he ceased, we sat with bowed heads as he withdrew. Our hearts were so enfolded, our souls so uplifted, our spirits so exalted, our whole being so permeated with his divinity, that when we arose we left the place silently and reverently, each bearing away a heart filled with higher, more divine aspirations, and clearer views of the blessed life upon which we were permitted to enter.

I can touch but lightly upon these heavenly joys. There is a depth, a mystery to all that pertains to the divine life, which I dare not try to describe; I could not if I would, I would not if I could. A sacredness enfolds it all that curious eyes should not look upon. Suffice it to say, that no joy we know on earth, however rare, however sacred, can be more than the faintest shadow of the joy we there find; no dreams of rapture, here unrealized, approach the bliss of one moment, even, in that divine world.[12]

EPILOGUE

I hope this journey down the typical believer's timeline has challenged you to do your utmost to detach yourself from earth life, and encouraged you to set your sights as high as the heavens which await you. I think you would agree that a grand subject such as this deserves a worthwhile response. When we consider God's enormous effort to rescue us from eternal doom and prepare us for heaven—with all its glorious realities—surely our reaction should be to consecrate ourselves anew to a life pleasing to Him!

What is your eternal destiny? It is to have every trace of flesh and sin removed from your inner being so that you can enjoy absolute union with Christ. It may be difficult to comprehend the utter bliss of that intimacy now, but when we arrive there, none of the other pleasures of heaven will compare with that.

I will conclude this book with these appropriate remarks from the apostle Peter:

> The day of the Lord is coming, and when it comes,
> it will be upon you like a thief. The heavens will vanish

in a whirlwind, the elements will be scorched up and dissolve, earth, and all earth's achievements, will burn away. All so transitory; and what men you ought to be! How unworldly in your life, how reverent towards God, as you wait, and wait eagerly, for the day of the Lord to come, for the heavens to shrivel up in fire, and the elements to melt in its heat!

And meanwhile, we have new heavens and a new earth to look forward to, the dwelling-place of holiness; that is what he has promised. Beloved, since these expectations are yours, do everything to make sure that he shall find you innocent, undefiled, at peace. (II Peter 3:10-14 Knox)

APPRENDIX ONE

BOOKS ABOUT VISITS TO HEAVEN

In an attempt to shed as much light as possible upon the believer's eternal destiny, I have, in the final section of this book, included testimonies (that I consider credible) from certain people who have had visions of heaven.

I did not do this in some misguided attempt to "juice" this book. Nor am I attempting to convince the reader that they should believe these accounts. Each of us must decide for ourselves what we believe about such things. My only purpose in including these stories has been to encourage the reader to look beyond the realm of sense. There *is* an unseen realm. There *is* a place called heaven. There *is* a realm beyond our temporal earth life. And whatever else might be said or believed about it, we can rest assured that it will be far better than the greatest human imagination could ever conceive. (I Corinthians 2:9)

With that understanding, allow me to comment on a few of these books.

"INTRA MUROS"

Rebecca Springer was born in Indianapolis in 1832, the daughter of a Methodist pastor. She graduated from the Wesleyan Female College in 1850. Nine years later she married an aspiring attorney who would later serve in the state legislature. Apparently she had a feeble constitution her entire life. It is unclear what year she had her after-death experience, but her book *Intra Muros** (Latin for "within the walls") was initially published in 1898.

The first time I gave any serious consideration to the subject of time

---

* It has been released by various publishers over the years, most recently by Baker Book House under the title of *My Dream of Heaven.*

and eternity was in 1993, when my spiritual mentor gave me a copy of *Intra Muros*. My initial impression of it was that the author was a very godly woman. It was mostly little things she said throughout the book that gave me that sense. I never had the feeling that it was conjured up or written for self-serving purposes. In the supplemental chapter, she wrote the following:

> I have never claimed that this strange experience is either a revelation or an inspiration. It came to me during a period of great physical suffering and prostration, and I have always considered it as sent in compensation for that suffering. Be this as it may, it has been a great comfort and help to me; and through the letters received from others, I am led to believe it has been the same to many who have read it, for which cause I am extremely gratified. I wish that I might give the entire experience just as it came to me, but I find that earth-language is wholly inadequate for me to do so. There were so many mysteries, so many teachings far beyond anything that in this life we have known, that I find myself bewildered and lost when I attempt to convey to others the marvelous things that at that time seemed indeed to me to be a most wonderful revelation.[1]

This little book paints such a vivid picture of heaven that I read it annually, just as a reminder of my eternal destination. As part of my research in writing my book, I went online to see what other readers had said about *Intra Muros* and was happy to find overwhelming support and praise for it. The readers who were most blessed by it were those who had lost loved ones. What a source of comfort and joy to be given such a realistic and true-to-life glimpse into that world of bliss which their beloved is now enjoying.

"VISIONS BEYOND THE VEIL"

For nearly fifty years H.A. Baker and his wife Josephine ministered to beggar boys in a Chinese town called Kotchiu. During the 1920s, they opened an orphanage there and took in forty of these boys. The Bakers regularly spent many hours in fervent prayer and one day, suddenly, the Holy Spirit came upon those children in a mighty way. While under the power of the Holy Ghost, they were allowed to experience the next world. It is an interesting side-note that the Bakers themselves were never given any of these visions. It is also worth noting that, prior to this experience, these children had received very little instruction about the hereafter. In fact, Mr. Baker wrote, "We did not teach these children about this Paradise. The children taught us. Some of the smallest children, who were naturally most ignorant of these matters, were our best teachers."[2]

"I SAW THE LORD"

Yet another person who has been entrusted with visions in the spiritual realm is a lady named Annie Schisler. I know her and her husband personally and have ministered in their church in Montevideo, Uruguay. Over a period of several months during the early 1970s, she too received a number of glimpses into the other world. She was a young woman who had just been born again and had no prior knowledge of the Bible, the evangelical realm or spiritual matters. I suspect that is why, like the Chinese boys, the Lord felt He could entrust such visions to her.

Her book of visions offers an extremely profound glimpse into the unseen realm around us. Although she occasionally received glimpses into the hereafter, she primarily was shown God's dealings with people from His perspective.

"HEAVEN"

Randy Alcorn's book is a theologically sound examination of the subject of heaven. I can understand why Stu Weber exclaimed, "Other than the Bible itself, this may well be the single most life-changing book you'll ever read."

Not only has he presented a very down-to-earth rendition of heaven, but he also accomplished some other important things along the way.

First, he exposed an errant perspective of heaven that he coins *Christoplatonism*. Basically, this false idea took root in the Early Church as certain Christian philosophers attempted to combine the mystical teachings of Plato (emphasizing immaterial things) with biblical concepts of heaven. *Christoplatonism* was the result: the belief that heaven is spiritual only, and as such, it will be devoid of any activity or even of time itself. Their notion of eternal life was a mundane existence devoid of any kind of activity. Alcorn insists that our eternity will be lived with physical bodies on a physical planet involved in physical activities. In other words, he dismisses the vague view of heaven the Church has held and presents a fresh perspective that our minds can actually grasp.

Another principle he points out in his book is that there is a difference between the present (or intermediate) heaven and the New Earth, where the saints will eventually spend eternity. His premise is that there is a temporary dwelling place called Paradise where deceased saints dwell until the Lord recreates earth. The New Earth will be somewhat like our current earth life, yet without any of the negative factors we associate with it: sin, strife, disease, decay, corruption and so on. Thus, his description of it is remarkably similar to life as we know it.

The last thing he accomplished in his book can best be summed up with the question he poses, "Why not?" He readily acknowledges that many of the scenarios he lays out are largely speculative, but the point he makes is that we know that anything God creates for our eternal happiness is only going to be good. "*Why can't it be like this?*" he asks. By and large our vague ideas about heaven have robbed Christians of one of the greatest motivators we can have to live a godly life. Randy's very plausible presentation about life in heaven is extremely compelling.

MISCELLANEOUS QUOTES AND VERSES PERTAINING TO TIME AND ETERNITY

QUOTES

"Who forces time is pushed back by time; who yields to time finds time on his side."—Talmud[1]

"Time is the wisest counselor of all."—Pericles[2]

"We all have our time machines. Some take us back, they're called memories. Some take us forward, they're called dreams."—Jeremy Irons[3]

"We know the past but cannot control it. We control the future but cannot know it."—Claude Shannon[4]

"This grand show is eternal. It is always sunrise somewhere; the dew is never all dried at once; a shower is forever falling; vapor is ever rising. Eternal sunrise, eternal sunset, eternal dawn and glowing, on sea and continues and islands, each in its turn, as the round earth rolls."—John Muir[5]

"Eternity! Thou pleasing, dreadful thought!"—Joseph Addison[6]

"Life is not lost by dying; life is lost minute by minute, day by dragging day, in all the thousand small uncaring ways."—Stephen Vincent Benet[7]

"We must wait until the evening to see how splendid the day had been."—Sophocles[8]

"Time cools, time clarifies; no mood can be maintained quite unaltered through the course of hours."—Mark Twain[9]

"The more sand that has escaped from the hourglass of our life, the clearer we should see through it."—Jean Paul Sartre[10]

"He who provides for this life but takes no care for eternity is wise for a moment but a fool forever."—John Tillotson[11]

"God does not always interpose in behalf of the innocent at once... however important time seems to us, it is of no consequence to God."—Albert Barnes[12]

"How can the past and future be when the past no longer is and the future is not yet? As for the present, if it were always present and never moved on to become the past, it would not be time but eternity."—Augustine[13]

"Our moments slip away silently and insensibly; time pursues his incessant course. Though we are listless and dilatory, the great measurer of our days presses on, still presses on, in his unwearied career, and whirls our weeks, and months, and years away."—Mr. Hervey[14]

"Time is but a fragment of eternity, and we obtain the best idea of it, perhaps, by standing on the banks of a mighty river; he beholds the flowing waters glide along in a powerful volume, taking complexion from all things round; he views the floating bubble, the fallen leaves, the scattered branches of trees, or various boats or living beings constantly borne away; he stands rapt in contemplation, not knowing what is above or what is below his vision, but he finds all life and time here imaged, vividly, and all rapidly pass away into the vast ocean of eternity."—J.G. Angley[15]

"Time never takes time off."—Augustine of Hippo[16]

"The characteristic thing about kairos is that it has to do with a definite point of time which has a fixed content...A divine decision makes this or that date a kairos, a point of time that has a special place in the execution of God's plan of salvation."—Oscar Cullmann[17]

"We all find time to do what we really want to do."—William Feather[18]

"There is no mortar that time will not loose."—French Proverb[19]

"Time heals what reason cannot."—Seneca[20]

"Enjoy the blessings of this day, if God sends them; and the evils of it bear patiently and sweetly: for this day only is ours, we are dead to yesterday, and we are not born to the morrow."—Jeremy Taylor[21]

"I know well enough what [time] is, provided that nobody asks me; but if I am asked what it is and try to explain, I am baffled."—Augustine[22]

"All my possessions for a moment of time."—Queen Elizabeth I, on her deathbed[23]

"Much may be done in those little shreds and patches of time which every day produces, and which most men throw away."—Charles Caleb Colton[24]

"Time is nothing to God."—Oswald Chambers[25]

"The great thing about time is that it goes on."—Arthur Eddington[26]

"History always repeats itself."—Proverb[27]

"Time, like an ever-rolling stream, bears all its sons away."—Isaac Watts[28]

"They say more people are laid low by *time anxiety* than by *time* itself. But only *time* is fatal."—Martin Amis[29]

"Time is the mediator between the possible and the actual."—G.J. Whitrow[30]

"That great mystery of TIME, were there no other; the illimitable, silent, never-resting thing called Time, rolling, rushing on, swift, silent, like an all-embracing ocean tide, on which we and all the Universe swim like exhalations, like apparitions which are, and then are not: this is forever very literally a miracle; a thing to strike us dumb—for we have no word to speak about it."—Thomas Carlyle c. 1840[31]

"The most useful men are often cut down by death, in the midst of their usefulness."—Jonathan Edwards[32]

VERSES:

"The Lord our God has secrets known to no one. We are not accountable for them, but we and our children are accountable forever for all that he has revealed to us, so that we may obey all the terms of these instructions." (Deuteronomy 29:29 NLT)

"The eternal God is a dwelling place, and underneath are the everlasting arms..." (Deuteronomy 33:27)

"The Eternal wrecks the purposes of pagans, he brings to nothing what the nations plan. The Eternal's purpose stands forever, and what he plans will last from age to age." (Psalm 33:10-11 Mof)

"Day by day the Lord takes care of the innocent, and they will receive an inheritance that lasts forever." (Psalm 37:18 NLT)

"So if you want an eternal home, leave your evil, low-down ways and live good lives." (Psalm 37:27 LB)

"For the Lord promotes justice, and never abandons his faithful followers.

They are permanently secure, but the children of evil men are wiped out."
(Psalm 37:28 NET)

"You have preserved me because I was honest; you have admitted me forever to your presence." (Psalm 41:12 LB)

"Your throne, O God, is forever and ever; a scepter of uprightness is the scepter of Your kingdom." (Psalm 45:6)

"He built His sanctuary like the heights, like the earth which He has founded forever." (Psalm 78:69)

"For I have said, 'Lovingkindness will be built up forever; in the heavens You will establish Your faithfulness.'" (Psalm 89:2)

"Your throne, O LORD, has been firm from the beginning, and you existed before time began." (Psalm 93:2 GNB)

"Your throne, O Lord, has stood from time immemorial. You yourself are from the everlasting past." (Psalm 93:2 NLT)

"You're blessed when you stay on course, walking steadily on the road revealed by GOD." (Psalm 119:1 MSG)

"Your word, O Lord, will last forever; it is eternal in heaven." (Psalm 119:89 GNB)

"Your kingdom is an everlasting kingdom, and Your dominion endures throughout all generations." (Psalm 145:13)

"When an evil man dies, his hopes all perish, for they are based upon this earthly life." (Proverbs 11:7 LB)

"Everything the Lord has made has its destiny; and the destiny of the wicked is destruction." (Proverbs 16:4 GNB)

"Everything has already been decided. It was known long ago what each person would be. So there's no use arguing with God about your destiny." (Ecclesiastes 6:10 NLT)

"Do not work for the food which perishes, but for the food which endures to eternal life, which the Son of Man will give to you..." (John 6:27)

"He said to them, It is not yours to know the chronological events in the passing of time nor the strategic, epochal periods of time which the Father placed within the sphere of His own private authority." (Acts 1:7 Wuest)

"The God who made the universe and all the things in it...marked out the limitations of strategic, epochal periods of time which have been appointed and the fixed boundaries of their occupancy..." (Acts 17:24-26 Wuest)

"For those whom He foreknew [*of whom He was aware and loved beforehand*], He also destined from the beginning [*foreordaining them*] to be molded into the image of His Son [*and share inwardly His likeness*], that He might become the firstborn among many brethren." (Romans 8:29 Amp)

"By his Spirit he has stamped us with his eternal pledge—a sure beginning of what he is destined to complete." (II Corinthians 1:22 MSG)

"For we know that if the earthly tent which is our house is torn down, we have a building from God, a house not made with hands, eternal in the heavens." (II Corinthians 5:1)

"For what is it we live for, that gives us hope and joy and is our proud reward and crown? It is you! Yes, you will bring us much joy as we stand together before our Lord Jesus Christ..." (I Thessalonians 2:19 LB)

"Tell those rich in this world's wealth to quit being so full of themselves and so obsessed with money, which is here today and gone tomorrow. Tell them to go after God, who piles on all the riches we could ever manage—to do good, to be rich in helping others, to be extravagantly generous. If they do that, they'll build a treasury that will last..." (I Timothy 6:17-19 MSG)

"You shared the sufferings of prisoners, and when all your belongings were seized, you endured your loss gladly, because you knew that you still possessed something much better, which would last forever." (Hebrews 10:34 GNB)

"Don't throw away your trust now – it carries with it a rich reward in the world to come." (Hebrews 10:35 PHP)

"By means of faith we perceive that the material universe and the God-appointed ages of time were equipped and fitted by God's word for the purpose for which they were intended, and it follows therefore that that which we see did not come into being out of that which is visible." (Hebrews 11:3 Wuest)

"Abraham did it by keeping his eye on an unseen city with real, eternal foundations—the City designed and built by God." (Hebrews 11:10 MSG)

"These men of faith I have mentioned died without ever receiving all that God had promised them; but they saw it all awaiting them on ahead and were glad, for they agreed that this earth was not their real home but that they were just strangers visiting down here." (Hebrews 11:13 LB)

"...they longed for a better country altogether, nothing less than a heavenly one. And because of this faith of theirs, God is not ashamed to be called their God for in sober truth he has prepared for them a city in Heaven." (Hebrews 11:16 PHP)

"So let us go out to him beyond the city walls [that is, outside the interests of this world, being willing to be despised] to suffer with him there, bearing his shame. For this world is not our home; we are looking forward to our everlasting home in heaven." (Hebrews 13:13-14 LB)

"God is in charge of deciding human destiny. Who do you think you are to meddle in the destiny of others?" (James 4:12 MSG)

"You have spent your years on earth in luxury, satisfying your every desire. You have fattened yourselves for the day of slaughter." (James 5:5 NLT)

"...we look forward to possessing the rich blessings that God keeps for his people. He keeps them for you in heaven, where they cannot decay or spoil or fade away." (I Peter 1:4 GNB)

"You call out to God for help and he helps—he's a good Father that way. But don't forget, he's also a responsible Father, and won't let you get by with sloppy living. Your life is a journey you must travel with a deep consciousness of God." (I Peter 1:17 MSG)

"Therefore, brethren, be all the more diligent to make certain about His calling and choosing you...for in this way the entrance into the eternal kingdom of our Lord and Savior Jesus Christ will be abundantly supplied to you." (II Peter 1:11)

"Dear brothers, you are only visitors here. Since your real home is in heaven, I beg you to keep away from the evil pleasures of this world; they are not for you, for they fight against your very souls." (I Peter 2:11 LB)

"The world is passing away, and *also* its lusts; but the one who does the will of God lives forever." (I John 2:17)

NOTES

PROLOGUE

1. Select choruses from "Shall We Gather at the River," a hymn by Robert Lowry (1826-1899).

INTRODUCTION

1. Joseph Parker, *Present and Future*, People's Bible Commentary, Reformed Church Publications.

CHAPTER ONE

1. Richter, *The Biblical Illustrator, Ephesians 5*, as cited in AGES Digital Library (Rio, WI: AGES Software, Inc., 2001) p. 164.
2. Ecclesiastes 3:11 New Living Translation.
3. *The American Heritage Dictionary of the English Language, Fourth Edition*, (Boston, MA: Houghton Mifflin Company, 2009).
4. *Cambridge Dictionaries Online*, accessed at http://dictionaries.cambridge.org/define.asp?key=time*1+0&dict=A on March 7, 2011.
5. Wikipedia, accessed at http://en.wikipedia.org/wiki/Time on February 28, 2011.
6. Nathan R. Wood, *The Secret of the Universe*, (New York, NY: Fleming Revel & Co., 1932) p. 44.
7. W.E. Vine, *Vines Complete Expository Dictionary of Old and New Testament Words* (Nashville, TN: Thomas Nelson, 1997) p. 279.
8. A.W. Tozer, *The Knowledge of the Holy*, (San Francisco, CA: Harper & Row, 1961) p. 67-68.
9. Charles Spurgeon, as quoted by Randy Alcorn in *Heaven*, (Carol Stream, IL: Tyndale House, 2004) p. 334.

CHAPTER TWO

1. Psalm 49:13-14 The Message.
2. Proverbs 14:8 Living Bible.
3. Steve Gallagher, *Intoxicated with Babylon*, (Dry Ridge: Pure Life Ministries, 2001) p. 213-214.
4. Alexander MacLaren, "The Rich Fool," *Luke 12*, Whole Bible Sermon Collection, as cited in AGES Digital Library (Rio, WI: AGES Software, Inc., 2001) p. 255.
5. John Milton, *Paradise Lost*, (New York, NY: Penguin Classics, 2003) p. 262.
6. John Wesley, "On Eternity," *Psalm 90*, Whole Bible Sermon Collection, as cited in AGES Digital Library (Rio, WI: AGES Software, Inc., 2001) p. 210.

CHAPTER THREE

1. Ecclesiastes 1:4 New Living Translation.
2. Philippians 2:15 New English Bible.
3. C. Short, *Pulpit Commentary, Psalm 12*, as cited in AGES Digital Library (Rio, WI: AGES Software, Inc., 2001) p. 11.

CHAPTER FOUR

1. Isaiah 38:18 The Amplified Bible.
2. Adam Clarke, *Adam Clarke's Commentary on the Bible, Proverbs 1*, as cited in AGES Digital Library (Rio, WI: AGES Software, Inc., 2001) p. 1602.
3. Charles Finney, "The Self-Hardening Sinner's Doom" a sermon preached May 9, 1849, accessed online at http://www.gospeltruth.net/1849OE/490509_sinners_doom.htm on March 7, 2011.

CHAPTER FIVE

1. Isaiah 55:6.
2. John Marsh, *Topical Encyclopedia of Living Quotations*, (Minneapolis, MN: Bethany House Publishers, 1982) p. 242.
3. Albert Barnes, *Albert Barnes Notes on the Bible, II Corinthians 4*, as cited in AGES Digital Library (Rio, WI: AGES Software, Inc., 2001) p. 702.
4. Charles Finney, *On Neglecting Salvation*, Master Christian Library, as cited in AGES Digital Library (Rio, WI: AGES Software, Inc., 2001) p. 991.
5. Beverly Carradine, *Remarkable Occurrences*, Master Christian Library, as cited in AGES Digital Library (Rio, WI: AGES Software, Inc., 2001) p.144.
6. *ibid.*, p. 147.
7. *ibid.*, p. 147.

CHAPTER SIX

1. Job 20:4-5 New Living Translation.
2. Philippians 2:15 Knox Translation.
3. Albert Barnes, *Albert Barnes Notes on the Bible, II Corinthians 4*, as cited in AGES Digital Library (Rio, WI: AGES Software, Inc., 2001) p. 667.
4. Martyn Lloyd-Jones, *Darkness and Light*, (Grand Rapids, MI: Baker Books, 1982) p. 41-42.
5. Martyn Lloyd-Jones, *God's Way of Reconciliation*, (Grand Rapids, MI: Baker Books, 1972) p. 112-113.

PART TWO

1. Jeremiah 10:23 Good News Bible.
2. J.D. Davies, *Pulpit Commentary, Ezekiel 7*, as cited in AGES Digital Library (Rio, WI: AGES Software, Inc., 2001) p. 30.

CHAPTER SEVEN

1. Hebrews 12:1-2 Moffatt.
2. W.E. Vine, *Vines Complete Expository Dictionary of Old and New Testament Words*, (Nashville, TN: Thomas Nelson Inc., 1997) p. 226.
3. Alexander MacLaren, "The Christian Life Race," *Hebrews 12*, Whole Bible Sermon Collection, as cited in AGES Digital Library (Rio, WI: AGES Software, Inc., 2001) p. 275.
4. Alexander MacLaren, "The Race and the Goal," *Philippians 3*, Whole Bible Sermon Collection, as cited in AGES Digital Library (Rio, WI: AGES Software, Inc., 2001) p. 119.

CHAPTER EIGHT

1. Psalm 90:10, 12 New Living Translation.
2. David Ravenhill, *Blood Bought: Rediscovering the Lost Truth of Our Redemption*, (prepublication).
3. C.H. Spurgeon, *The Biblical Illustrator, I John 2*, as cited in AGES Digital Library (Rio, WI: AGES Software, Inc., 2001) p. 97.
4. Beverly Carradine, *The Blessings of Time*, Master Christian Library, as cited in AGES Digital Library (Rio, WI: AGES Software, Inc., 2001) p. 133.
5. Canon Diggle, *The Biblical Illustrator, I John 2*, as cited in AGES Digital Library (Rio, WI: AGES Software, Inc., 2001) p. 91.
6. Anonymous, *Inspiring Quotations; Contemporary and Classical*, (Nashville, TN: Thomas Nelson Inc., 1988) p. 204.

CHAPTER NINE

1. Benjamin Franklin, *Inspiring Quotations; Contemporary and Classical*, (Nashville, TN: Thomas Nelson Inc., 1988) p. 204.
2. Ephesians 5:15-17 J.B. Phillips translation.
3. A. T. Pierson, *The Biblical Illustrator, Ephesians 5*, as cited in AGES Digital Library (Rio, WI: AGES Software, Inc., 2001) p. 155.
4. Henry Longfellow, as quoted by Paul Davies in *About Time*, (New York, NY: Simon & Shuster, 1995) p. 13.
5. Jonathan Edwards, "The Precious Importance of Time and the Importance of Redeeming It," *Ephesians 5*, Whole Bible Sermon Collection, as cited in AGES Digital Library (Rio, WI: AGES Software, Inc., 2001) p. 1382.
6. Henri Fredric Amiel, *Inspiring Quotations; Contemporary and Classical*, (Nashville, TN: Thomas Nelson Inc., 1988) p. 203.
7. Lord Chesterfield, accessed at http://www.jatland.com/forums/showthread.php?17361-Quotes....../page5 on March 14, 2011.
8. J. Stoughton, *The Biblical Illustrator, Ephesians 5*, as cited in AGES Digital Library (Rio, WI: AGES Software, Inc., 2001) p. 168.

CHAPTER TEN

1. Psalm 88:9 NKJV.
2. Anonymous, *Inspiring Quotations; Contemporary and Classical*, (Nashville, TN: Thomas Nelson Inc., 1988) p. 204.
3. Antoinette Bosco, *Inspiring Quotations; Contemporary and Classical*, (Nashville, TN: Thomas Nelson Inc., 1988) p. 203.
4. Oswald Chambers, *Oswald Chambers, The Best from All His Books, Vol. I*, (Nashville, TN: Thomas Nelson Inc., 1988) p. 359.
5. A.W. Tozer, *Root of Righteousness*, (Camp Hill, PA: Christian Publications, 1956).
6. S.D. Gordon, *Quiet Talks on Prayer*, (Grand Rapids, MI: Baker Book House, 1980) p. 12, 150.
7. An Unknown Christian, *The Kneeling Christian*, (Grand Rapids, MI: Zondervan Publishing Co., 1971) p. 17.
8. E.M. Bounds, *E.M. Bounds on Prayer*, (Baker Book House, Grand Rapids, MI, 1981) p. 95, 147.
9. Leonard Ravenhill, *Revival Praying*, (Minneapolis, MN: Bethany House, 1962).

CHAPTER ELEVEN

1. Romans 8:18 J.B. Phillips translation.
2. Charles Spurgeon, "The Trial of Your Faith" a sermon delivered December 2, 1888 at the Metropolitan Tabernacle, Newington, CT, accessed online at: http://www.spurgeongems.org/vols34-36/chs2055.pdf on March 2, 2011.
3. Oswald Chambers, *The Best From All His Books*, (Nashville, TN: Thomas Nelson Inc., 1989) p. 110.

PART THREE

1. Anonymous, *Inspiring Quotations; Contemporary and Classical*, (Nashville, TN: Thomas Nelson Inc., 1988) p. 204.
2. J. Flavel, *The Biblical Illustrator, Ephesians 5:16*, as cited in AGES Digital Library (Rio, WI: AGES Software, Inc., 2001) p. 166.
3. I Timothy 4:8 Living Bible.
4. Psalm 50:3-4 Good News Bible.

CHAPTER TWELVE

1. II Corinthians 9:9 Living Bible.
2. Alexander MacLaren, "Redeeming the Time," *Ephesians 5*, Whole Bible Sermon Collection, as cited in AGES Digital Library (Rio, WI: AGES Software, Inc., 2001) p. 238.
3. Dwight Moody, "Heaven," Whole Bible Sermon Collection, as cited in AGES Digital Library (Rio, WI: AGES Software, Inc., 2001) p. 124.

CHAPTER THIRTEEN

1. Tom Stoppard, accessed at http://www.finestquotes.com/select_quote-category-Explanation-page-2.htm on March 14, 2011.
2. Psalm 51:5a, 10, 12 The Message.
3. Steve Gallagher, *Intoxicated with Babylon*, (Dry Ridge: Pure Life Ministries, 2001) p. 193.
4. S. Conway, *Pulpit Commentary, Revelation 22*, as cited in AGES Digital Library (Rio, WI: AGES Software, Inc., 2001) p. 39.

CHAPTER FOURTEEN

1. G. Calthrop, *The Biblical Illustrator, II Corinthians 5*, as cited in AGES Digital Library (Rio, WI: AGES Software, Inc., 2001) p. 100.
2. Philippians 1:11 New Living Translation.
3. Glenn Meldrum, *Rescue Me—Finding Freedom Through Godly Character*, (Covert, MI: Wisdom's Gate Publishing, 2007) p. 23.

CHAPTER FIFTEEN

1. Martin Luther, accessed at http://www.goodreads.com/quote/show/203914 on March 14, 2011.
2. Psalm 37:18 Living Bible.
3. W.B. Godbey, *Commentary on the New Testament, I Corinthians 3*, Master Christian Library, as cited in AGES Digital Library (Rio, WI: AGES Software, Inc., 2001) p. 39.

4. Alexander MacLaren, "Two Builders on One Foundation," *The Biblical Illustrator, I Corinthians 3*, as cited in AGES Digital Library (Rio, WI: AGES Software, Inc., 2001) p. 159.
5. Beverly Carradine, *The Better Way*, Master Christian Library, as cited in AGES Digital Library (Rio, WI: AGES Software, Inc., 2001) p.71.
6. Randy Alcorn, *Heaven*, (Carol Stream, IL: Tyndale House Publishers, 2004) p. 232.
7. Rene Pache, as quoted by Randy Alcorn in *Heaven*, (Carol Stream, IL: Tyndale House Publishers, 2004) p. 220.

PART FOUR
1. Rebecca Ruter Springer, *Intra Muros* (re-titled *My Dream of Heaven*), (Tulsa, OK: Harrison House, 2002) p. 102.

CHAPTER SIXTEEN
1. Psalm 41:13 Living Bible.
2. Isaac Watts, a hymn entitled "Great God, How Infinite Art Thou!" access at http://www.readbookonline.net/readOnLine/35337/ on March 14, 2011.
3. John Wesley, *On Eternity*, Whole Bible Sermon Collection, as cited in AGES Digital Library (Rio, WI: AGES Software, Inc., 2001) p. 205.
4. A.W. Tozer, *Knowledge of the Holy*, (Camp Hill, PA: Christian Publications, 1961) p. 64.
5. *ibid.*
6. John Wesley, *On Eternity*, Whole Bible Sermon Collection, as cited in AGES Digital Library (Rio, WI: AGES Software, Inc., 2001) p. 209.

CHAPTER SEVENTEEN
1. Psalm 37:10-11, 34 Moffatt Translation.
2. Revelation 21:4 The Amplified Bible.

CHAPTER EIGHTEEN
1. Romans 14:17 New Living Translation.
2. Isaiah 51:11.
3. Charles Spurgeon, *The Best of C.H. Spurgeon*, (Grand Rapids, MI: Baker Book House, 1989) p. 46.
4. Charles Finney, "The Rich Man and Lazarus," *Luke 16*, Whole Bible Sermon Collection, as cited in AGES Digital Library (Rio, WI: AGES Software, Inc., 2001) p. 830.
5. George Ritchie, M.D., *Return From Tomorrow*, (Grand Rapids, MI: Chosen Books, 1978) p. 48-49.
6. Rebecca Ruter Springer, *Intra Muros* (re-titled *My Dream of Heaven*), (Tulsa, OK: Harrison House, 2002) p. 11-13.
7. Betty Maltz, *My Glimpse of Eternity*, (Wiltshire, England: Spire Books, 1977) p. 84-88.
8. W.F. Adeney, *Pulpit Commentary, Jeremiah 32*, as cited in AGES Digital Library (Rio, WI: AGES Software, Inc., 2001) p. 41.
9. A.W. Tozer, *After Midnight*, (Camp Hill, PA: Christian Publications, 1959).

CHAPTER NINETEEN

1. Revelation 21:2 Living Bible.
2. Joni Erickson Tada, as quoted by Randy Alcorn, *Heaven*, (Carol Stream, IL: Tyndale House Publishers, Inc., 2004) p. 294-295.
3. Randy Alcorn, *Heaven*, (Carol Stream, IL: Tyndale House Publishers, Inc., 2004) p. 78.
4. H.A. Baker, *Visions Beyond the Veil*, (New Kensington, PA Whitaker Books: 1973) p. 69-70.
5. Rebecca Ruter Springer, *Intra Muros* (re-titled *My Dream of Heaven*), (Tulsa, OK: Harrison House, 2002) p. 88-90.
6. Randy Alcorn, *Heaven*, (Carol Stream, IL: Tyndale House Publishers, Inc., 2004) p. 411-412.
7. *ibid.*, p. 423-425.
8. Rebecca Ruter Springer, *Intra Muros* (re-titled My Dream of Heaven), (Tulsa, OK: Harrison House, 2002) p. 28-29.
9. H.A. Baker, *Visions Beyond the Veil*, (New Kensington, PA Whitaker Books: 1973) p. 54, 70.
10. Billy Graham, *Angels*, (Dallas, TX: Word Publishing, 1975) p. 69-72.
11. R. Edward Miller, *I Saw the Lord, Book One: Annie's Visions*, (Montevideo, Uruguay: Ediciones Peniel, 1974) p. 19-20.
12. Rebecca Ruter Springer, *Intra Muros* (re-titled *My Dream of Heaven*), (Tulsa, OK: Harrison House, 2002) p. 63-67.

APPENDIX ONE

1. Rebecca Ruter Springer, *Intra Muros* (re-titled *My Dream of Heaven*), (Tulsa, OK: Harrison House, 2002) p. 127-128.
2. H.A. Baker, *Visions Beyond the Veil*, (New Kensington, PA Whitaker Books: 1973) p. 67.

APPENDIX TWO

1. Talmud, accessed at http://www.quotegarden.com/time.html on March 10, 2011.
2. Pericles, accessed at http://www.quotegarden.com/time.html on March 10, 2011.
3. Jeremy Irons, accessed at http://thinkexist.com/quotation/we_all_have_our_time_machines-some_take_us_back/346041.html on March 10, 2011.
4. Claude Shannon, accessed at http://www.usc.edu/uscnews/stories/15212.html on March 10, 2011.
5. John Muir, accessed at http://www.finestquotes.com/author_quotes-author-John%20Muir-page-0.htm on March 10, 2011.
6. Joseph Addison, accessed at http://quotationsbook.com/quote/39075/#axzz1GDaLyMu3 on March 10, 2011.
7. Stephen Vincent Benet, accessed at http://thinkexist.com/quotation/life_is_not_lost_by_dying-life_is_lost_minute_by/179167.html on March 10, 2011.
8. Sohphocles, accessed at http://www.goodreads.com/quotes/show/29214 on March 10, 2011.
9. Mark Twain, accessed at http://www.quotationspage.com/quote/1645.html on March 10, 2011.

10. Jean Paul Sartre, accessed at http://www.justquoted.com/quote/The-more-sand-that-has-escaped-from-the-hourglass-.htm on March 10, 2011.

11. John Tillotson, as quoted by Randy Alcorn, accessed online at http://www.epm.org/resources/tag/judgment/ on March 9, 2011.

12. Albert Barnes, *Albert Barnes' Notes on the Bible, Psalm 37:7*, accessed online at http://bible.cc/psalms/37-7.htm on March 9, 2011.

13. Augustine, as quoted by Paul Davies in *About Time*, (New York, NY: Simon & Shuster, 1995) p. 70.

14. Hervey, *The Biblical Illustrator, Ephesians 5:16*, as cited in AGES Digital Library (Rio, WI: AGES Software, Inc., 2001) p. 166.

15. J. G. Angley, *The Biblical Illustrator, Ephesians 5:16*, as cited in AGES Digital Library (Rio, WI: AGES Software, Inc., 2001) p. 152-153.

16. Augustine of Hippo, *Topical Encyclopedia of Living Quotations*, (Minneapolis, MN: Bethany House Publishers, 1982) p. 241.

17. Oscar Cullmann, *Topical Encyclopedia of Living Quotations*, (Minneapolis, MN: Bethany House Publishers, 1982) p. 242.

18. William Feather, *Topical Encyclopedia of Living Quotations*, (Minneapolis, MN: Bethany House Publishers, 1982).

19. French Proverb as quoted in *Topical Encyclopedia of Living Quotations*, (Minneapolis, MN: Bethany House Publishers, 1982) p. 242.

20. Seneca, *Topical Encyclopedia of Living Quotations*, (Minneapolis, MN: Bethany House Publishers, 1982) p. 242.

21. Jeremy Taylor, *Topical Encyclopedia of Living Quotations*, (Minneapolis, MN: Bethany House Publishers, 1982) p. 242.

22. Augustine, *Inspiring Quotations; Contemporary and Classical*, (Nashville, TN: Thomas Nelson Inc., 1988) p. 203.

23. Queen Elizabeth I, as quoted in *Inspiring Quotations; Contemporary and Classical*, (Nashville, TN: Thomas Nelson Inc., 1988) p. 203.

24. Charles Caleb Colton, accessed at http://www.goodreads.com/quotes/show/318235 on March 11, 2011.

25. Oswald Chambers, *Oswald Chambers, The Best from All His Books, Vol. I*, (Nashville, TN: Thomas Nelson Inc., 1988) p. 359.

26. Arthur Eddington, as quoted by Paul Davies in *About Time*, (New York, NY: Simon & Shuster, 1995) p. 25.

27. Proverb as quoted by Paul Davies in *About Time*, (New York, NY: Simon & Shuster, 1995) p. 36.

28. Isaac Watts, as quoted by Paul Davies in *About Time*, (New York, NY: Simon & Shuster, 1995) p. 252.

29. Martin Amis, as quoted by Paul Davies in *About Time*, (New York, NY: Simon & Shuster, 1995) p. 255.

30. G.J. Whitrow, as quoted by Paul Davies in *About Time*, (New York, NY: Simon & Shuster, 1995) p. 275.

31. Thomas Carlyle, as quoted by Dan Falk in *In Search of Time: The Science of a Curious Dimension*, (New York, NY: St. Martin's Press, 2008).

34. Jonathan Edwards, *Procrastination*, Whole Bible Sermon Collection, as cited in AGES Digital Library (Rio, WI: AGES Software, Inc., 2001) p.1401.

INTOXICATED WITH BABYLON

The strength of *Intoxicated with Babylon* is Steve Gallagher's sobering deliverance of the unvarnished truth to a Church rife with sensuality and worldly compromise. In a time when evangelical Christians seem content to be lulled to sleep by the spirit of Antichrist, *Intoxicated with Babylon* sounds a clarion wake-up call in an effort to draw the Body of Christ back to the Cross and holy living. Those with itching ears will find no solace here, but sincere believers will experience deep repentance and a fresh encounter with the Living God.

IRRESISTIBLE TO GOD

Before a person can come into intimate contact with a Holy God, he must first be purged of the hideous cancer of pride that lurks deep within his heart.

"This book is a road map that shows the arduous but rewarding way out of the pit of pride and into the green pastures of humility. Here is the place of blessing and favor with God."—Steve Gallagher

Humility is the key that opens the door into the inner regions of intimacy with God. *Irresistible to God* unfolds the mystery that God is indeed drawn to the one who is crushed in spirit, broken by his sin, and meek before the Lord and others.

AUDIO CDs

BREAKING FREE FROM THE POWER OF LUST

Many Christians break out of the habits of outward sin but feel as though their thought lives will never change. However, the Lord has given answers that work. In this series Jeff Colón examines the key biblical principles that, when applied to one's life, break the power of lust in the believer's heart. (4 CD SET)

GOD'S CALL TO REPENTANCE

Repentance was the cry of the prophets in the Old Testament, the message of John the Baptist in the New Testament, and Jesus' repeated admonition to the churches in Revelation. It remains the indispensable heart-condition of every true believer. With deep gratitude for what God did in his own life, Pastor Jeff Colón issues a call to repentance that seems to flow right from the heart of God. Application messages draw from the lives of King David and King Saul to contrast the life-changing impact of true repentance. [4 CD SET]

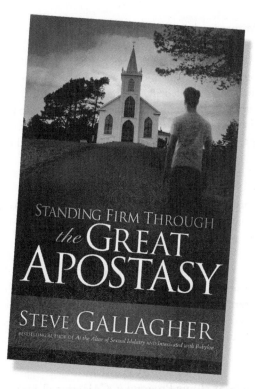

THE IMPLICATIONS OF THIS BOOK ARE TERRIFYING.

In this thorough, and sometimes disquieting, investigation of biblical predictions, the Great Apostasy emerges, not as a foreboding future event, but as the very essence of today's postmodern Church.

Like tares in the wheat field, false adherents are presently growing up alongside true believers. But how will we know them? What are the distinguishing qualities of these apostate confessors?

This is where Steve Gallagher is at his best. By mining the treasure-laden writings of past centuries and carefully examining the sacred Scriptures, he exposes the prevailing self-centeredness, widespread sensuality, and rebellion to authority that epitomizes this false part of the Body.

Be prepared for your perspective of the End Times Church to be forever changed.

PURE LIFE MINISTRIES

Pure Life Ministries helps Christian men and women achieve lasting freedom from sexual sin. The Apostle Paul said, "Walk in the Spirit and you will not fulfill the lust of the flesh." Since 1986, Pure Life Ministries (PLM) has been discipling Christians into the holiness and purity of heart that comes from a Spirit-controlled life. At the root, illicit sexual behavior is sin and must be treated with spiritual remedies. Our counseling programs and teaching resources are rooted in the biblical principles that, when applied to the believer's daily life, will lead him out of bondage and into freedom in Christ.

BIBLICAL TEACHING RESOURCES

Pure Life Ministries offers a full line of books, audio CDs and DVDs specifically designed to give Christians the tools they need to live in sexual purity.

RESIDENTIAL CARE

The most intense and involved counseling PLM offers comes through the **Live-In Program** (6-12 months), in Dry Ridge, Kentucky. The godly and sober atmosphere on our 45-acre campus provokes the hunger for God and deep repentance that destroys the hold of sin in men's lives.

HELP AT HOME

The **Overcomers At Home Program** (OCAH) is available for those who cannot come to Kentucky for the Live-In program. This twelve-week counseling program, which is also available for struggling women, features weekly counseling sessions and many of the same teachings offered in the Live-In Program.

CARE FOR WIVES

Pure Life Ministries also offers help to wives of men in sexual sin. Our wives' counselors have suffered through the trials and storms of such a discovery and can offer a devastated wife a sympathetic ear and the biblical solutions that worked in their lives.

PURE LIFE MINISTRIES

14 School St. • Dry Ridge • KY • 41035
Office: 859.824.4444 • Orders: 888.293.8714
info@purelifeministries.org
www.purelifeministries.org